Good Practice Guide: **Marketing your Practice**

RIBA Good Practice Guides

Other titles in this series:

Building Condition Surveys, by Mike Hoxley

Employment, by Brian Gegg and David Sharp

Extensions of Time, by Gillian Birkby, Albert Ponte and Frances Alderson

Fee Management, by Roland Phillips

Inspecting Works, by Nicholas Jamieson

Keeping Out of Trouble, by Owen Luder

Mediation, by Andy Grossman

Negotiating the Planning Maze, by John Collins and Philip Moren

Painless Financial Management, by Brian Pinder-Ayres

Starting a Practice, by Simon Foxell

Good Practice Guide: Marketing your Practice

Edited by **Helen Elias**

RIBA ⊞ **Publishing**

Published by RIBA Publishing, 15 Bonhill Street, London EC2P 2EA

ISBN 978 1 85946 307 9

Stock Code 69154

British Library Cataloguing-in-Publication Data
A catalogue record for this book is available from the British Library.

Publisher: Steven Cross
Commissioning Editor: James Thompson
Editor: Helen Elias
Project Editor: Alasdair Deas
Designed by Ben Millbank
Typeset by Academic + Technical
Printed and bound by MPG Books, Cornwall

RIBA Publishing is part of RIBA Enterprises Ltd.
www.ribaenterprises.com

Series foreword

The *Good Practice Guide* series has been developed specifically to provide architects, and other construction professionals, with practical advice and guidance on a range of topics that affect them, and the management of their business, on a day-to-day basis.

All the guides in the series are written in an easy-to-read, straightforward style. They are not meant to be definitive texts on the particular subject in question, but each guide will be the reader's first point of reference, offering them a quick overview of the key points and then providing them with a 'route map' for finding further, more detailed information. Where appropriate, checklists, tables, diagrams and case studies are included to aid ease of use.

Good Practice Guide: Marketing your Practice

Competition for work is a sign of a healthy industry, and competition in the construction industry is today as intense as it has ever been. In the face of the combined challenges of economic recession, new procurement routes, competitive pricing and ever more sophisticated clients, every architectural practice should aim to maximise its chances of standing out from the crowd.

To do so, architects must take a professional and organised approach to selling the services they provide. This admirable *Good Practice Guide* shows how to do exactly that. Avoiding jargon, it makes clear from the outset how marketing goes hand-in-hand with developing a greater understanding of your practice's strengths, of your clients' needs and of the broader opportunities out there.

This is the key message of the book: successfully marketing an architectural practice is about much more than simple promotional activity. It is about taking a considered approach to growing your practice, positioning yourself within the industry, communicating your vibrancy and developing new business. All of these are vital to the health of any business, and I recommend that all practices think about them, and take time to implement them creatively.

Ruth Reed
President, RIBA

Preface

All architects, whether they like it or not, operate within the professional services sector. An architectural practice wins its work and builds its reputation upon the creativity, passion and ability of the people that it employs.

Differentiation, brand awareness and reputation are the intangible assets that attach themselves to successful firms. Each practice has to set out its stall to attract clients. Planning across business development, communication and branding is essential, as is getting it right from day one for a fresh new practice seeking to make its mark in the world. First impressions count, and nowhere more so than in an industry which is based upon design.

Those firms that have thought carefully about what they stand for, and that have developed a considered approach to the presentation of their work, will inevitably be more attractive to client organisations looking to spend their money wisely.

The world of architecture has always been a buyer's market, but this is especially the case in the current highly competitive commercial climate. Every practice claims to offer a passion for design, creativity, innovation, a sustainable approach, dedicated teams and thought leadership. Every practice says that it listens to the client, and exceeds expectations. So, following a submission and presentation process, why should a client organisation chose one practice over another?

The commercial marketplace is currently governed by long-term uncertainty. Against this background, cost-effective, targeted marketing is going to play a vital role in the success, possibly even the immediate survival, of some architectural practices. This guide is for directors and partners of existing and new architectural practices, who aspire to maximise the effectiveness of their marketing and new business efforts. A group of key experts who specialise in marketing, business development, design and communication for the built environment sector have collaborated to share their thinking, exploring the core issues that, together, contribute to the way any architectural firm positions itself in the market. There is a lot to say and, when it comes to successfully marketing architecture in a crowded market with diminishing client opportunity, there is a lot to do.

Helen Elias
December 2009

About the authors

Editor

Helen Elias, editor of and contributor to this book, has spent her career working within the built environment sector as a journalist, marketing communications manager and independent communications consultant. Currently Marketing Director, Building Engineering, with AECOM, Helen also writes for key industry journals, and is the author of *Effective Press Relations for the Built Environment: A Practical Guide* (Taylor & Francis, 2006).

Contributors

Section 1 – Caroline Cole is founder of Colander (www.colander.co.uk), a consultancy which works across the built environment sector to help firms develop their business and management skills, so that they can maintain a profitable balance between creative excellence and business acumen.

Section 2 – Judith Powling and Julie Fitzsimmins are founding directors of Lodestar Marketing (www.lodestaruk.com), providing specialist advice in marketing strategy, planning and implementation to the construction and property sector, as well as to industry bodies and professional organisations, in the UK and Europe.

Section 3 – Roy Kent is the founder of Kent Strategic Marketing Solutions (www.kentsms.com), specialising in business development consultancy for the built environment.

Section 4 – David Grossmann is a director of Basler & Hofmann. With thanks to MarketingWorks (www.marketingworks.co.uk) for strategic process mapping.

Section 5 – Michele Jannuzzi is a founding partner of the London-based design consultancy Jannuzzi Smith (www.jannuzzismith.com).

Section 7 – John Foster is Managing Director of Shere Marketing (www.sheremktg.co.uk) and Charmaine Kimpton is an account manager for the firm, which has provided expert marketing and PR services to the built environment sector since 1989.

Section 8 – David Crawford, managing partner of Technical Editorial Consultancy (Dandecrawford@btconnect.com), is a technical writer, researcher and communicator specialising in the built environment and transport.

Section 10 – Alex Harvie is a publishing and writing consultant (www.alexharvie.com). With thanks to Gustafson Porter and Sheppard Robson for their assistance and to Black Dog Publishing and Thames and Hudson for their time.

Acknowledgement

With thanks to Trudy Evans, Spratley Studios, for the example press release (Appendix 1).

Contents

Section 1
Marketing: setting a direction for the practice

Caroline Cole, *Colander*

The RIBA accredits around 3300 chartered practices. Of these firms, around 75 per cent employ ten or fewer people. This means that many architects work in practices that are too small to justify employing people simply to manage the business and look after the marketing side of things. As a result, when it comes to marketing the business, and finding the projects where the designers most want to deliver creative work, many architects have to do it themselves.

Synergy between architects and marketing

Remember, architects are not in business to sell widgets. Although architects ultimately create a product – usually a building – they are equally selling a service, working alongside the client and others to achieve the product.

This means selling the individual skills, expertise, imagination and enthusiasms of professionals to people who, in the main, have a special project that they believe needs dedicated, individual attention.

This suggests that a successful marketing strategy will build on the personal enthusiasms and expertise of the people in the practice and will find ways of promoting these skills to the outside world. However, it is extremely difficult to deliver such a strategy unless there is a close synergy between a practice's marketing efforts and the architects who deliver the goods. If architects associate marketing with unwanted sales pitches, or treat it as an add-on to their core business, to be delegated to non-fee earning staff, then this synergy is unlikely to be achieved.

So, how can marketing become an integral part of an architectural practice? How can architects become inspired to contribute to the marketing efforts? Quite simply, marketing has to embrace architecture. It has to involve activities that motivate architects and in which they want to participate. It has to allow architects to communicate with the world as professionals, not as sales staff, and it has to relate clearly to the practice's architectural vision and ethos.

If the marketing strategy for an architectural practice cannot rise to this challenge, then it will have failed.

While generating new business may be the ultimate aim, marketing can and should go well beyond the activities that are directly associated with bidding for new work; it should be as much about building the reputation of the practice in the marketplace; in other words, establishing a position in the market.

Marketing has two main goals:

1 To attract the right clients with the right projects to the practice.
2 To attract the right staff and support services to ensure that the firm can deliver the projects that it wins, to the highest standards.

To do this successfully it is important to understand – and articulate – what is meant by: 'right clients', 'right projects', 'right staff' and 'highest standards'. Without this understanding, it will be impossible to put together a marketing strategy that will help the practice to develop according to the aspirations of the founding architects.

In other words, it is important to first understand why the practice is in business to start with. From that starting-point it is easy to articulate what to sell and to whom. Then, and only then, can the firm put together a marketing strategy to determine how to achieve its business aims (Figure 1.1).

This means that the key to a successful marketing strategy is to start with a robust vision or business plan for the practice.

Creating a business plan

It is important to recognise that business planning takes real time. It is not something that can be done by one person at evenings and weekends. If it is to be

FIGURE 1.1: *The business aims of an architectural practice must inform its marketing strategy*

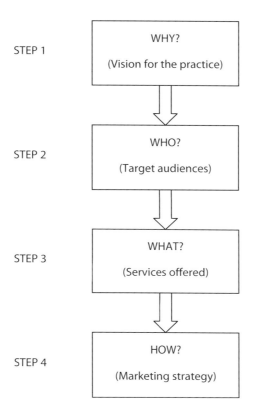

STEP 1

WHY?

(Vision for the practice)

STEP 2

WHO?

(Target audiences)

STEP 3

WHAT?

(Services offered)

STEP 4

HOW?

(Marketing strategy)

effective, then it must include contributions from all key members of the practice, culminating in a sense of consensus and ownership from everyone who will be expected to deliver the desired end results.

To start, two things must be clarified:

1   Where the firm is today.
2   Where the firm wants to be in, say, five years' time.

All elements of the business need to be considered (Figure 1.2):

FIGURE 1.2: *Consider all elements of the business when creating a business plan for the practice*

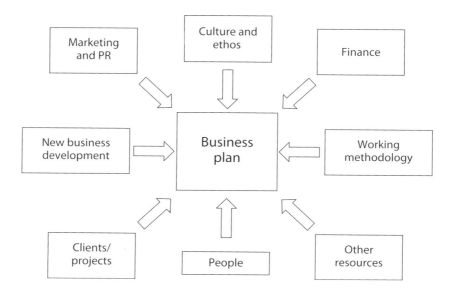

- Culture and ethos: what is the character of the practice, what is its management style?
- Clients and projects: what kind of clients do the teams want to work with, on what kinds of projects (include scale and location)?
- Working methodologies: how do the teams want to work?
- People: what kind of people does the firm want to employ and what skills should they have?
- Finance: what are the financial aspirations for the business?
- Marketing and new business development: who needs to know about the practice and what reputation does the firm want to have in the marketplace?
- Other resources: what other resources does the business need to achieve its aims – premises, IT and so on?

Where is the practice today?

Start by understanding where the business is now – this will ensure a realistic appreciation of what needs to be done to achieve the practice's long-term aims. An assessment of the current position of the business can helpfully be divided into internal and external issues.

Internal issues

- What are the current commitments – short-term (less than a year), medium-term (two to three years) and long-term (four years and over)?
- What have been the trends in the practice over past three years – financial, staff levels, project size and type, successes, failures, awards, other achievements?
- What services does the firm offer – consultancy/advisory, architectural, other professional services, and so on?
- What resources are already to hand – money, time, premises, skills, management and staff?
- What are the strengths and weaknesses of the practice – internal issues, over which the leaders have control?

External issues

- What are the opportunities and threats to the practice – external influences, over which the firm has no control? Consider political, economic, social, technological and environmental issues.
- What are the external perceptions of the practice? Undertake a review to gauge external perceptions and understand the potential that the practice has, in the eyes of the outside world. Don't just ask clients, talk to other consultants, contractors, client advisers, industry pundits and the competition.

Where does the practice want to be?

Don't just think about aspirations for the coming year, or for the year after, because this will only address short-term issues.

Instead, look at the long term. Assume it is five years from now and pretend to describe the practice to a journalist. What does the practice want to have achieved over the past five years?

- What kind of projects have been built and where?
- What kind of clients does the firm now work for?
- What kind of people are employed and how many of them are there?
- What reputation has been established?
- What role are the founding partners now playing in the practice?

It is important that the aspirations for the business are founded on the individual aspirations of the key people involved in the practice, so they should all contribute. The plan will not be successful if it does not reflect consensus. It is critical that all are committed to the agreed actions, with a common focus, achieved through consultation.

Most importantly, broad agreement needs to be reached on the firm's target market and portfolio, and the motivation for those choices, before any further progress can be made.

Who is the target market?

The question to ask here is: 'Who needs to know what about my practice?' Target audiences will not be confined to clients. Consider also:

- industry leaders
- other professional consultants
- potential partners
- contractors
- other architects
- students.

It is probably true to say that a practice that delivers good, professional work will cause targeted clients to come to the firm of their own accord. Certainly, this concept is corroborated by the Colander benchmark surveys of the architectural profession, which show that, year on year, at least one-third of clients rely on personal recommendations as part of their selection process. Happy clients give confidence and reassurance to potential new clients. Unhappy clients can undo months of careful selling with a single shrug of the shoulders.

"Happy clients give confidence and reassurance to potential new clients."

There are two main ways that existing clients can help new business efforts: by giving the firm repeat business and by becoming part of the firm's sales team.

Repeat business

It is surprising how many practices forget to sell to their existing clients and yet, referring again to the Colander benchmark surveys, almost 70 per cent of practices rely on repeat business for 50 per cent or more of their new business, with the most profitable practices recording, on average, around 80 per cent of their new business from repeat clients.

This emphasis on existing clients is interesting because:

• current clients are easier to woo, because a relationship already exists
• marketing costs are lower, particularly in terms of non-chargeable time
• new work from existing clients should be more profitable
• it is easier to pass work from repeat clients to more junior fee-earners because these clients already know and trust the practice
• it creates a hugely effective marketing tool to reassure and attract new clients
• it forces the practice to identify core strengths and helps to create a stable foundation for the firm's brand.

However, it should be remembered that a practice that relies only on repeat business is putting its business at risk since:

• there may be little potential for more work from existing clients
• there is a real danger for a company which has all its eggs in one basket
• new clients and new opportunities are stimulating and help practices to retain good staff.

Client as ambassador

If a firm's clients are satisfied with the work delivered, they are likely to become unconscious ambassadors for the practice. By telling colleagues and business connections about the good work provided by the firm, they are effectively selling on the firm's behalf. To encourage clients to act as ambassadors, they need to be given:

• excellent projects, of which they are rightly proud
• excellent service, so they enjoy working with the practice
• a continuing relationship, so they have the practice at the forefront of their minds
• up-to-date information about the firm's current work and future aspirations
• the opportunity to sing the praises of the practice, so invite them to events.

New clients

Architects are trained to believe that they can solve all architectural challenges, so they have a natural inclination to think – and therefore to say – 'I can do anything for anyone'.

However, in this age of specialisation, more often than not, clients want an expert. They ask for 'examples of similar buildings' and a 'proven track record' to give assurance that the architects they are considering bring the required expertise to the table. If the practice does not have a track record of successfully delivered buildings, it will need to find other ways of convincing new clients that this firm of architects is worth considering.

"clients want an expert"

To do this, the practice needs to consider itself as a problem solver rather than a product developer; then sell itself accordingly. Go back to the idea that the business is not just selling a product – or building – but also selling a service. It is highly likely that the service already delivered to existing clients is similar to that required by the new client. So, consider ways of packaging 'service expertise' and skills so as to interest targeted clients.

When deciding what the firm wants to sell and to whom, over the next five years, consider the matrix in Figure 1.3.

FIGURE 1.3: *Matrix defining services offered and routes to clients*

Services offered ⟶	
Existing services to existing clients	New services to existing clients
Existing services to new clients	New services to new clients

A new practice with a few established clients will sit in the top left-hand square. If, in five years' time, the partners want, say, 20 per cent of all business to come from the bottom right-hand square, then a route must be planned through the other squares to achieve this aim. Existing work and tried and tested skills can be used to help make each move.

What does the firm want to sell?

In his 1999 paper outlining the future strategy for the RIBA, called 'Meeting the Challenge: Repositioning the Profession', architect Roger Zogolovitch stated that: 'the fundamental strength of the architect is the ability to interpret and direct the shape of our environment through the process of design'.

This is not something that project managers can do. This is the special 'added value' that architects have to offer, encompassing the iconic model put forward by Roman architect Marcus Vitruvius. Writing in about 20–30 BC, Vitruvius believed that an architect should focus on three central themes when preparing a design for a building: *firmitas* (strength/commodity), *utilitas* (functionality) and *venustas* (beauty/delight), shown in Figure 1.4.

The problem is that many clients do not really understand what services an architect can offer, or where an architect is best able to 'add value'. Asked to rank their requirements in order of importance, most clients will put design quality well down their list. Service-related issues come at the top of the list:

- ability to deliver the project on time
- ability to deliver within budget
- ability to listen, to take and develop a brief
- ability to work with others, as a team member – to lead the design team
- ability to make presentations on behalf of the client.

FIGURE 1.4: *The Vitruvian model*

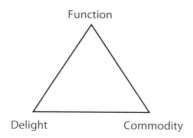

While clients find it difficult to articulate their feelings when it comes to design quality, they are very able to distinguish between what they regard as an 'excellent' as opposed to an 'acceptable' service.

However, any well-trained technician or project manager can deliver a project to time and budget. So, while these attributes are clearly required, they are unlikely to make one architectural firm stand out from the crowd, or necessarily make the best use of an individual's skills and talents as an architect, and as a professional.

The question therefore is rather complex. How can a firm of architects inspire clients to take the plunge and invest, possibly to buy something that they are not aware that they need until it is given to them? It helps to step back and look at the bigger picture: clients don't want an architect, they want a solution to their problems.

Step into the client's shoes and define the services that they need. Then decide on the following:

- If the practice were to offer any additional services, would that increase its ability to sell core architectural services?
- Does the practice have the skills to offer these services in-house, or will it need to buy them in, or find collaborators?

For example, consider the following services:

- At the front end: site finding, brief writing, stakeholder consultations and design quality indicator (DQI) facilitation, optioneering, feasibility studies and evaluations, master planning, planning advice or client representation.
- During the project: engineering, sustainability advice, cost control, lighting design, landscape design, interior design, wayfinding.
- At the back end: post-occupancy evaluations, user manuals, space planning and relocation management.

The client's comfort zone

The key to successful marketing is being able to think like clients, demonstrating an understanding of the issues that clients are facing within their sector.

All architects need to have a passion and an enthusiasm for the building types being undertaken by the clients from whom they are seeking work. This means having knowledge and understanding of the problems, or challenges, that those building types pose. If there is nobody in the practice with an interest in, let alone a passion for, the type of work being chased, then the firm is highly unlikely to win that work. Taking a position in any market by default means that the practice wants to generate further business in that sector. If clients are not convinced about the practice's knowledge and market position, new business will be harder to come by.

The practice needs to get under the skin of the client:

- What are the client's aspirations?
- What are the client's fears?
- What constraints is the client working under?
- Where does the client see their opportunities, both personally and corporately?
- How does the client measure their successes and their failures?
- How will the client measure their architect's successes and failures?

So, how can a practice find these things out about a client?

First, be prepared to listen. Then, be ready with the right questions. However, to do either of these things, the partners need to meet the right people, in the right setting and at the right time. The following sections consider possible approaches.

User groups

Invite a group of people, possibly from different client organisations, to discuss the practice's performance in a certain area. Outline to them how and why certain working methods were adopted, talk about plans for improving service. Then invite their comments.

Reverse seminars

Invite, say, the chief executive of a major client to come and talk to the firm about a subject that is pertinent to his or her sector. Consider inviting colleagues from other consultants to attend: favourite engineers, quantity surveyors, agents or even other clients.

Undertaking research

Identify topics that are important to clients and the sector in which they work but that are also of interest to the practice and its architects – and which will enhance the quality of the work that can be created. Such research might look at technical issues (new materials, sustainability issues, use of colour in buildings) or it might address broader issues relating to wider client concerns (off-site construction, standardisation, how improved environments can enhance productivity).

Choose the topics carefully, as research can offer many opportunities to engage with clients:

- carrying out the research provides an excuse to contact client organisations that might not otherwise be willing to talk
- once the research is completed, it provides an excuse to contact the same people again, to present the findings.

Most importantly, this approach gives the opportunity to engage with clients on an equal footing, not as a salesperson.

Attending sector meetings or conferences

Conferences can be used to listen and learn. Consider offering to take one of the firm's respected clients to such an event, to learn from their comments. Don't just confine attendance to architectural conferences, also attend events that address the broader aspects of a client's working environment and industry sector.

Reading the right magazines

Each client sector will have technical and trade press – just as the architectural profession does. Read the right magazines to understand the key issues that are affecting the way in which potential clients do business.

Join networking groups and institutions

Each client sector has various networking groups set up specifically to help people across the construction industry to meet other like-minded people, be they others on the supply side or clients. Get involved in the management of these groups – or join one of the numerous panels across the industry that look at different aspects of the built environment. Contribute to local cross-industry networking organisations, or to panels set up by those in government – both local and central.

Project team debriefings

Use team debriefings to collect feedback from the client, not only at the end of the project but on a continuous basis. Many clients do similar reviews for their own businesses, so why not for the architect? Equally, think about how to get feedback from designers, and how this feedback is collated, reacted to and further disseminated around the practice.

Client, consultant and peer group surveys

As already mentioned, client surveys are a useful tool as part of business planning. However, they are also good for collecting information about how and what clients think: about the practice and also about the world in which they work.

Ask about the practice – for example:

- Why was, or was not, the practice appointed to projects?
- Feedback on performance – by the practice and by individuals.
- What are the perceived strengths and weaknesses of the practice?
- Would people would like to work with the practice again, or recommend the firm?
- What makes the practice special?

But ask also about the world in which they work:

- What do they see their main challenges to be in the coming years?
- What are the main blocks and the main drivers for their businesses?
- What do they expect from their architects at the moment – and how might that change in the future?
- How could the practice serve them better?
- Who are the main competitors – and why?

Client surveys can be undertaken formally or informally, by the practice or through an intermediary. The important thing is to get honest and constructive answers from the clients.

"get honest and constructive answers from the clients"

These methods of listening to the client are important when establishing the position of a practice within any market sector because:

- the firm can learn from them
- feedback can drive improvements to service
- they help to identify new opportunities
- they enable the practice to find out about competitors
- they strengthen the client relationship.

Usefully, from a marketing and new business point of view, each of these activities can be used as a selling tool in its own right and, critically, architects are more likely to be interested in getting involved as they can see a direct correlation between these activities and their ability to deliver effective architecture.

Each of these activities will increase knowledge about client organisations and the world in which they operate. However, they will also help to build the practice's own reputation and brand within the marketplace; so, in effect, they are fundamental marketing and brand-building activities.

Finding the time

Any successful marketing strategy will include management and administrative tasks. There is a well-worn business adage that says: what you do with your billable time determines your current income, but what you do with your non-billable time determines your future.

A good rule of thumb is that the principals in a practice should be spending, on average, one-and-a-half days per week on their business. To check this, analyse the number of hours actually billed to clients against the number of hours spent at work. It is very likely that principals will spend more than one-and-a-half days per week on non-billable time.

Consider a system that divides time into three areas:

1 Project time: billable hours.
2 Personal time: training, regeneration, etc.
3 Investment time: marketing, business planning, etc.

Plans, programmes and monitoring systems will be in place for dealing with project time. Put in place similar procedures for planning and monitoring the investment time – with defined tasks and a time-scale attached to each.

Marketing activities can usefully be divided into three groups:

1 Bidding activities: time and money attributable to specific project opportunities, including competition entries.
2 Specific marketing activities: all non-bidding, marketing and promotional activities which can be attributed to specific clients.
3 Non-specific marketing activities: all non-bidding, marketing and promotional activities which cannot be attributed to specific clients.

The percentage allocated to each of these activities will vary depending on the specifics of the marketing plan. However, if one activity is dominating, then this will merit review.

In investment time, think about whether the firm is up to speed with client needs:

• What can the practice do to help clients further? Are there new services that should be offered?
• How can new client contacts be turned into long-term client relationships?
• How can the practice earn unprompted referrals from existing clients?
• What is being done to ensure that the right people in each market area are aware of the capabilities of the practice?
• How good are the principals at turning inquiries into real projects? What do they need to do better?
• Is the company attracting the right kind of new recruits?
• How could project work be delivered more cheaply?

Achieving a successful architecture practice

It is a challenge to run a successful practice – one that creates wealth for happy people, involves interesting projects, delivers exceptional buildings to delighted clients and, ultimately, establishes a good reputation that engenders pride and satisfaction.

One of the main reasons why success can be so elusive is that architects like being architects; few are inspired by business management and therefore few will devote the same time and energy to running their businesses as they do to designing projects.

So, do not set up an architectural business without being prepared to spend a significant percentage of personal time focusing on the needs of the business, rather than simply enjoying the pleasures of being an architect. To give a rule of thumb, if a principal in practice works 1700 hours a year, no more than 1200 to 1400 hours should be spent on fee-earning work. This leaves around a day-and-a-half per week on non-billable time: time to spend developing and nurturing the business.

SUMMARY

- Understand why the practice is in business and establish what it can offer to clients.
- Create a long-term business plan.
- Sell the practice's skills and imagination and promote its professional service delivery.
- Identify and understand all target audiences, undertaking research to ensure a thorough understanding of the marketplace.
- Listen to clients in order to build client relationships, encouraging feedback on completed projects and the practice's perceived strengths and weaknesses, and actively seek repeat business.
- Ensure that sufficient time is devoted to non fee-earning work to nurture business development.

Section 2
Marketing strategy: from planning to delivery

Judith Powling and Julie Fitzsimmins, *Lodestar Marketing*

Marketing strategy is about translating business plans, business objectives and aspirations into reality. A business plan is the master plan for the architectural practice. Whether managing the process internally or with external help to establish the business plan, the aim is always to develop a plan that will drive conclusions and actions. Business plans provide a robust platform from which to develop marketing strategy and plans, but so many business plans end up on the shelf, gathering dust. Ensure that your practice's business plan is revisited regularly and kept alive; question the plan and review it, so that it does not become set in stone, intractable and unwieldy.

Generally, not just in architectural practices, but across construction and other sectors, relatively few business plans are developed. Where they do exist, businesses tend to put the plans on the shelf and launch straight from the business plan (having ticked the box for the benefit of the bank or investors) to developing 'marketing' in the shape of promotional literature and media relations.

What makes it difficult to implement business planning and marketing strategy development? In smaller businesses it is usually due to the necessity of getting on with the day job and not having specific marketing expertise within the business, but it is also to do with the tendency to 'go with the flow' when times are good. We see more reflection in periods of downturn. However, this reflection can often be too late, as businesses are not fully aware of their own

FIGURE 2.1: *Strategy – planning – implementation*

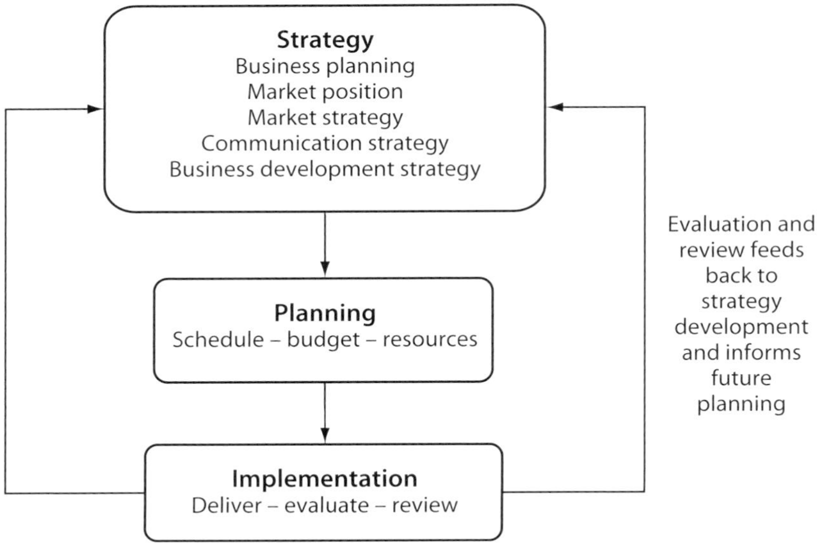

make-up, strengths and sources of key turnover, let alone the status of the firm's pipeline of work and the length of time needed to build and develop relationships to lead to new work. Practices with a dedicated 'marketing person' will frequently keep that key staff member concentrating on tender and pitch documents, websites and literature, exhibitions and events, and media relations. This approach, focused on delivery, is great, but, nine times out of ten, that delivery is not part of a coherent plan informed by a strategy.

The danger here is that marketing and communication are ad hoc and not part of a plan developed from a business strategy. This is risky. Precious resources can be wasted, and mixed and inconsistent messages can be sent to clients and other stakeholders. The activities can also be hard to manage, making their effectiveness even harder to measure in order to justify the investment. As marketing is a cost centre, it has to justify itself within the business (Figure 2.1).

Developing a marketing strategy

Marketing strategy, in its most simple terms, is about understanding how to position architectural services in the marketplace in order to deliver business objectives and create profit. There are key areas to explore, research and capture.

This process presents a great opportunity to develop an understanding of the marketplace, gain inspiration and think about how best to grow or consolidate the business. A clear process helps to ensure that plans are based on something rigorous and meaningful, not just plucked from the air. It creates core information that can be shared with, and easily understood by, colleagues within the practice.

Working with colleagues to develop a marketing strategy

Share the research and information-gathering activity between partners, directors or associates, or ask the marketing specialist in the practice to manage the exercise. Some firms appoint an external expert to help drive the process and analysis. Individuals that already lead on particular sectors or business areas should drive forward the work on their sector.

Set a time-frame that fits around the day-to-day work of the practice. Meet regularly, and ensure that each meeting has agreed key deliverables so people know what they are being expected to bring or discuss.

Importantly, secure senior level buy-in to ensure that findings and recommendations are supported. Ensure that a champion supports this work at practice board meetings. Set a date for presenting and sharing the information, this provides an impetus to complete the work.

The marketing strategy will develop through addressing two fundamental areas:

- market position, and
- market strategy.

These provide an informed and solid base from which a communication strategy and plan, or business development strategy and plan, or both, can be developed, depending on what is already in place and what the business needs (Figure 2.2).

The first step is to determine *market position*. Building on the framework described in Section 1, this is the process of identifying the practice's position in the marketplace, in comparison to its competitors, and identifying a strategic approach to the marketplace. Ultimately, this enables the practice to be clear

FIGURE 2.2: *Marketing process*

about what it needs to communicate, and to whom. It keeps the principals focused on the firm's offer and services and what the implications for clients and associated stakeholders are. It leads, very naturally, to the development of a communication strategy and plan.

Market position areas to review are:

- clients
- SWOT (strengths, weaknesses, opportunities and threats)
- competitors
- communication.

Client review

Many companies carry out aftercare questionnaire evaluations with their clients. This often focuses solely on the project itself, but it is important to take into account clients' views of the organisation as a whole. How do clients perceive the practice? What are the needs and challenges of current and potential clients? Understanding clients' needs and their views of the practice helps to focus the way in which the firm currently delivers work and highlights areas on which to focus in the future. It can even help to identify new added value elements that are prized by clients.

Action

- Consult with clients, past and present and potential.
- Develop a standard range of questions, for example:
  - What is the client experience of the practice?
  - Why do they choose to work with the practice?
  - How would they describe the practice as an organisation?
  - How does the practice compare with competitors/the sector as a whole? (It can be helpful to add a means of measurement against specific factors here.)
  - What challenges are there in clients' current supply chains?
  - How could clients work with the practice in the future?
  - Is there anything that clients would like the practice to do that is currently not offered?
  - Take the opportunity to discuss where the industry is going and the clients' biggest concerns. What do clients think are the major opportunities in the future and how could the architectural sector change to work more effectively with clients in the future?
- Develop and record this through telephone or face-to-face meetings, evaluation forms or client feedback sessions and then bring the information together so it can be analysed and discussed and then actions and responsibilities decided.
- Aggregate the information and present it to the board as a current view of the practice.
- Use the information to develop a written strategy by extracting key points: the practice's strengths and the aspects of what the practice does that differentiate it from competitors.

This information can then be used to inform a SWOT analysis.

SWOT – helping to differentiate the business

SWOT analysis focuses on internal issues:

What are the practice's:	Strengths
	Weaknesses
What/where are:	Opportunities
	Threats

FIGURE 2.3: *SWOT analysis*

STRENGTHS	WEAKNESSES
• What does your practice do really well? • What do others see as your strengths? • Do you have particular sector or market knowledge? • Why do clients commission you?	• What could you improve? Service? Profile? Client follow-up? • What might others see as your weaknesses? • What reasons mean you have not secured a tender or commission?
• What knowledge/experience do you have that you could promote to other markets or sectors? • Are there policy changes that could provide an opportunity for your skills or services? • What trends are you aware of?	• Challenges? Risks? • Competitors – are you aware of what your competitors are doing? • Are market needs changing?
OPPORTUNITIES	THREATS

SWOT is a really useful tool to focus minds on what the practice is good at. The most important thing is to identify and understand the factors, and then to review and assess the implications and consequences for the business (Figure 2.3).

Be honest and open when it comes to the weaknesses and the threats; equally, push hard on what constitute the practice's key strengths. For example, a strength might be environmental knowledge – is that because of a particular specialist on the team, a particular area of knowledge, has someone been involved in policy development, or is it due to a string of successful projects which have demonstrably improved environmental performance? Strengths are what set the practice apart, what differentiate it and make the business the right choice for clients. It is vital to spend time working out why the practice's services and skills make it stand head and shoulders above competitors and then to capture this knowledge, which can be used to inform the development of the practice's messages and also to identify areas of growth and development for the business.

Action

- Set out the results of the SWOT analysis in a table – capturing the strengths and then considering the implications or consequences of those strengths ensures that this work is not superficial.
- Mine data collected during the consultation with clients. Capture opinions about the firm in the SWOT.
- Create action plans, particularly around the weaknesses and threats that are uncovered by the analysis.

Competitor analysis: helping to differentiate the business

Competitor analysis is created by desk-based research and by sharing knowledge about the firm's competitors. Basic intuitive and anecdotal knowledge about competitors will exist, drawn from tender situations, meetings at industry events, media coverage and looking at which firms win key awards. On unsuccessful pitches, go back to the client and ask who won the work, and try to discover what made the difference between the pitches.

Competitor analysis is fundamental to business growth and understanding of market share. Who has the larger share? How can the practice win more? Understanding what the firm is up against in existing and new markets is essential to driving success.

Action

- Combine desk research (web search and information gathering) with brain-storming or knowledge-sharing meetings. This creates a solid reference resource that can help to develop messaging, brand and corporate identity (see Section 5, *Branding an architectural practice*).
- Interview key staff to gather market intelligence.
- Take a structured approach to collecting information: compile it into tables – what do competitors do?; services, sectors, specialisms – how do they describe them?
  - How do competitors present themselves – size, length of time in business, key messages, sectors, specialisms?
  - How do they present their brand – visual and verbal?
  - What projects have they won?

○ How does all of this compare with what the practice currently offers and the way it presents itself to the market?

○ If possible, determine how the practice is positioned compared to its competitors. Illustrating this in a diagram or graph will aid internal communication.

• Determine the practice's share of the key markets and assess what potential share could be won.

Communication audit

An audit is a very practical way of reviewing how the practice is currently presenting itself to the market. This process often highlights some interesting issues: for example, messages may be inconsistent, brand may be applied in different ways, colours, positioning, etc. There may even be out-of-date materials that are still in use. Auditing communication materials on a regular basis is similar to undertaking an annual MOT or health check, as well as forming part of the groundwork for strategy development.

Action

• What communication materials exist – print, website? Are they doing their jobs?

• Do all materials present the practice brand consistently, both visually and verbally?

• What are the current messages being communicated? Are they consistent? Do they truly reflect the business? Do they differentiate the firm or are just saying the same as everyone else?

• How did they compare with competitors' marketing collateral during competitor analysis?

• Do the visuals and photography reflect the messages?

• Review the practice's strengths from the SWOT. Are these reflected in the language, case studies and angles that are presented? Are there gaps?

Market strategy

Market strategy is the firm's approach to the markets in which it actively operates. Clearly, this is related to its market position. Strategy and position inform each other and, while it is important to consider them separately, they are not separate silos. Market strategy is informed by knowledge gathered about preferred markets or sectors. Actions include:

- researching the market
- documenting understanding of chosen markets
- developing stakeholder analysis of organisations to target
- developing approaches to sectors.

These activities will provide the fundamentals for a business development strategy and plan.

Market strategy areas to consider include the following:

1 Review the practice's current offer and services offered to its markets.
2 Marketplace research: examine key market trends and influences.
3 Who are the key stakeholders?

Review the firm's current offer and services offered to its markets

Reviewing services offered and active markets and sectors gives a clear picture of what the practice is doing, and where the work is being done. The review may find that particular high value front-end work is being successfully delivered in one sector but not in another. The review can also identify opportunities to cross-sell services to other markets, sectors and clients, and identify potential sectors to develop, all of which will form the business development strategy and plan.

Action

- Markets. Review how the practice currently breaks down the markets in which it operates. Which services are offered to which markets? Do they have to be adjusted for different markets?
- Services. Map and review each area of the business by the services offered, by sectors and by clients. How does turnover break down by service? What is the turnover and profitability? Are there some services that are highly profitable? What does this say about the business? Can services be packaged together to leverage and secure bigger projects or different clients? This area of review identifies opportunities of selling particular services to particular clients and, by extension, to particular markets or sectors.

- Sectors. Focus on which sectors the practice already works in, what services are offered, and the turnover and profitability by sector. Some sectors may turn over significant volume but create little profit. This allows the business little headroom, but perhaps gives critical profile in particular sectors. Other drivers for keeping less profitable work may be that it attracts excellent people or helps to retain existing staff.
- Can the practice cross-sell between sectors or to certain clients?
- Identify and agree targets for particular services or sectors to fulfil the turnover and profitability objectives set out in the business plan or gap analysis.
- Identify any cross-sectoral themes, such as regeneration or sustainability. Themes enable experience and expertise to be grouped for a range of different potential clients and stakeholders. They provide a context for discussions and positioning the practice, as well as 'hooks' for the practice's communication strategy and communication plans within different sectors.

Marketplace research: examine key market trends and influences

What knowledge exists within the practice about its markets? How is this knowledge shared around the practice? Most practices have a great deal of knowledge, but it is not shared or used to develop strategy except in an ad hoc way. Marketplace research, combined with analysis of current services, will enable identification of sectors or markets to focus on and will provide factual data on which to base decisions. This will provide the strategic direction for the business development plan.

Action

- A combination of brainstorming, desk research and knowledge-sharing meetings will provide the back-up needed to make informed decisions. External expertise can help to facilitate this exercise. Consult practice-wide. Consider making it a team activity, asking everybody to bring examples, information, facts and web-research outputs to a knowledge-sharing meeting. Giving everybody a chance to contribute can be a good team-building exercise.
- Establish a process to share market knowledge gleaned from industry media, web RSS feeds and other sources; for example, forwarding items around the team or assigning individuals a responsibility to extract summary information and circulate weekly digests. Create 'Market' folders within the practice's shared folders to which people can save information.

FIGURE 2.4: *PEST(LE) analysis*

POLITICAL	ECONOMIC	LEGAL
• Government – political impacts • Political change – national, regional, local • Trade controls – overseas markets • Rapid change could create threats/opportunities	• Economic picture – interest rates, inflation • Labour market – supply, demand, costs • Economic change and forecasts • Tax policy – change or stability?	• Regulation/legislation and impacts of change, i.e. Part L • Could this impact on products or materials you specify? • Changes in taxation • Could changes in health and safety or employment law affect the practice?
• Demographic profiles • Lifestyle change • Population patterns • Health, employment – changes and attitudes • Cultural trends • Press and public opinion	• Impact of emerging technologies • R&D activity – external and internal • Impacts of increased remote working • Likelihood of technological change?	• What are the environmental factors that affect the business and its clients • How is climate change likely to impact upon your clients? • Ethical sourcing of materials • Biodiversity and site issues
SOCIO-CULTURAL	TECHNOLOGICAL	ENVIRONMENTAL

- Undertake PEST(LE) (political, economic, social and technological (plus legal and environmental)) analysis to look at the external factors influencing the practice, markets or sectors (Figure 2.4). PEST(LE) is a useful tool for understanding the big picture, drivers for change and consequent potential impacts on the business. Developing PEST(LE) analysis by sectors or markets also helps to develop understanding of client marketplaces and the threats and opportunities in their sectors that might affect business with individual clients. Used regularly, it provides a structured way of assessing change and impacts. PEST(LE) is also particularly useful for planning how to break into a new country or a new sector.
- What are the opportunities resulting from market trends or the current situation in a particular market? Feed this information into the SWOT analysis.
- Develop a sector-based framework or template for sector leaders to store current sector information. Identify the opportunity and record actions, these can feed into the business development strategy and plan.

Who are the practice's stakeholders?

Stakeholder mapping can be undertaken sector by sector and to plot contacts within individual client organisations. It is a fundamental and invaluable tool for understanding who to communicate with.

- *Primary stakeholders (decision-makers)* – the priority contacts that make the ultimate decisions in relation to purchasing services. A client as end-user, a developer, an investor or a contractor as client could all be primary stakeholders. Break down primary stakeholders into groups with a common agenda. For example, a FTSE 100 client usually has a different agenda to that of a private investor.
- *Secondary stakeholders (influencers)* – who influence the primary stakeholders. Secondary stakeholders can include other architects, engineers, project managers, QSs, cost consultants, contractors, planners and even lawyers.
- *Tertiary stakeholders (market influencers)* – the people and organisations that influence the market and the policies that affect the markets.

First steps are to look at the existing current sectors and potential sectors and 'map' the relevant stakeholders. This process often highlights gaps in people's knowledge in terms of who the practice should be targeting in order to develop new business, and those individuals with whom it would be politic to develop relationships to create a positive climate for decision-making in relation to a particular project. Often, this process highlights the fact that a contact base is very thin and a more robust process of developing better relationships with decision-makers or influencers would be prudent.

Stakeholder mapping is a fundamental process that provides a solid basis for the business development plan, which is about engaging closely with individuals, and for the communication strategy and plan, which focus more on corporate communication and communicating more broadly.

Action

- List the current and potential companies or organisations and then prioritise them. This begins to build the stakeholder map and identify target lists.
- If the map includes large generic groups – for example, project managers may be a critical secondary stakeholder to growing business in retail – identify the companies and specific individuals.
- Apply this approach to the sectors in which the practice currently works, set out the sector top ten for each group, then set out the practice's top ten

and compare the lists. Is the practice in touch with all of the sector top ten? Which organisations are priorities?

Pulling it all together: planning and implementation

This groundwork gives a clearer idea of the firm's market position – where it is in the marketplace – and will inform market strategy. This will enable the practice to target markets effectively by playing to the practice's perceived strengths via clear communication and business development strategies, and plans that will easily develop from the research and market knowledge developed through this process.

Communication strategy and planning

Drawing on market position, and particularly the stakeholder mapping from the market strategy development, the communication strategy will focus on the following points:

- Who does the firm want to communicate with?
- What are the key messages for the principal stakeholder groups?
  - Primary messages: what the practice is about, value added areas, perception.
  - Secondary messages: reassurance for clients that the practice is what they need.

Developing messaging

Drawing from the SWOT analysis and client consultation, identify the unique selling proposition (USP) that sets the practice apart from other architects.

- How can the practice be described?
- What are the practice values?
- What really matters to the people in the firm?
- How are these values relevant to clients?
- What is the unique message? Fulfilling basic client expectations, such as delivering to time and to budget, need to be covered but they are not primary messages.

Even well-known, established businesses can face communication difficulties if they do not have a clear proposition that can be readily understood by their clients and staff. The dreaded 'elevator pitch' may be marketing speak, but it

FIGURE 2.5: *Messaging matrix*

Messaging			Target audiences (indicate relevance for that audience)								
Message *What is it that you want to convey?*	**Objective** *What is the objective of this message?*	**Rationale** *The supporting story for this message – how can you evidence this?*	Domestic	Retail	Leisure	Sport	Heritage	Workplace	Transport	Education	Health
		Project examples Client quote Statistics Images			✓	✓	✓			✓	

does capture the essence of a short description of the business and what it does – quick enough to convey to someone while travelling together in a lift to the next floor! In networking situations those who can relay what their practice does in a compelling and concise way have a winning combination. This does not require a sales pitch but something short (around 30 seconds) that is sufficiently inspiring or engaging to stimulate further discussion. Ensure that it is focused on why the firm's approach is unique in providing value and benefit to clients. This value proposition statement overarches all messaging. Test it out on your team, and even on some particularly close clients.

Market position, client profile and target markets or sectors will heavily influence messaging. Take account of audiences' differing needs in the messaging developed – domestic residential audiences need a different approach from that used for commercial clients. Setting out the messages in a matrix will clarify what to say to which groups, and provide a structure and discipline for setting out the rationale that supports each message (Figure 2.5).

Communication planning

Communication plans are the outputs from the research and strategy. They are developed to support and deliver business objectives. Communication plans ideally provide a year-long programme that is scheduled and costed, with responsibilities indicated. Developing plans on a sector-by-sector basis provides focus, but it is vitally important to coordinate all plans to take account of overarching corporate communication activity and potential overlap in audiences between different sectors.

For example, one key contact, say a project manager working with the firm in three sectors, could end up receiving three separate mailings or invites, wasting practice resources and giving a poor impression of the practice's efficiency. Internal systems for key account management (KAM) and customer relations management (CRM) are critical for managing contact relationships. PC- or Apple-based systems are available that do not cost the earth and can help to coordinate efforts. However, these systems are only as good as the data entered and the consistency of approach. Alternatively, a spread-sheet is straightforward and easy to use and can provide an 'at a glance' summary of the year, with detailed costed plans sitting behind in subsequent worksheets.

So, for example, a firm with a focus on developing themes of sustainability and regeneration and a business development strategy to drive forward growth within retail and the workplace might have an outline communication plan resembling that shown in Figure 2.6.

Business development strategy and planning

Preparing a business development strategy ensures careful thought about business development targets. It is no good just being busy – the effort has to work towards delivering.

Start by deciding on the practice's approach to business development. Is KAM a key approach for developing new business? Is sector-based business develop-ment the key strategy? Or is it a combination of both?

Developing new business with new clients is generally estimated to cost ten times as much as developing business with existing clients. If 80 per cent of turn-over is coming from 20 per cent of clients, clear plans are needed to involve and engage these critical stakeholders over an agreed time period.

As KAM is a process for managing key client relationships, it should include account reviews and client development plans as part of that process. KAM is

FIGURE 2.6: *Outline communication planning*

Monthly activity	Description	Jan	Feb	Mar	April	May	June	July	Aug	Sept	Oct	Nov	Dec
Corporate profile	External events Media Newsletter Practice events		Practice stakeholder newsletter	MIPIM	Practice stakeholder newsletter			Practice stakeholder newsletter			Practice stakeholder newsletter		
Sector: Retail	Theme development ICSC, BCSC, MAPIC				ICSC Euro Conf							MAPIC & BCSC	
Sector: Workplace	Develop sector research BCO	BCO Annual Dinner								BCO Awards	BCO Lunch		
Theme: Sustainability	Develop "expert" columns												
Theme: Regeneration	Develop regeneration forum			Forum devt →						Forum 1	Link to Thames Gateway Forum	Link to BCSC Conf/ Exh	
Target audiences/ stakeholders	Developers Investors End-users Local authority clients												

also a practical way of developing new business from existing contacts by using the network as a basis for generating new contacts.

Action

- The business development strategy should set out the business development financial objectives.
- Establish and agree business development objectives that relate to the target groups, key accounts and sectors and the method of measurement for each objective.
- Develop a brief summary of the approach to business development over a pre-determined period. Why are specific areas being targeted? What is being offered?
- Select the priority target groups from the stakeholder mapping. Agree a strategic approach to each target.
- Follow this with an action plan that sets out what is going to be done by when and by whom.

As well as thinking about business development strategies and plans, consider how this work could be supported by product development within the business and in marketing communication activity. Ensure that this is understood so that the marketing communication budget is focused on addressing business development targets.

Marketing communication

At its most basic level, in many practices marketing communication supports business development by pulling together tender and bid submissions and ensuring there is appropriate marketing communication collateral in print or online, and sometimes by developing corporate entertainment. The marketing communication team or person should be able to contribute marketing activity that supports business development and develop communication plans that engage key targets. Ensure that your marketing team understands the practice's targets and that they are focused on the groups that will deliver business in the future.

For instance, to drive forward growth within retail and the workplace, with a focus on the themes of sustainability and regeneration, marketing might organise a detailed action plan for the practice at key industry exhibitions and conferences, such as MAPIC, MIPIM, BCO and BCSC. The plan would aim to communicate the practice's key themes and focus on business development targets. It should include setting up meetings for the principals at the events and might include hosting lunches and dinners, with key target contacts being invited. It is vital to capture all data gathered promptly on return from the event, carry out a review with all those involved and issue follow-up materials. Consider supporting event attendance through online media such as a Twitter or a live feedback blog on the practice's website.

Evaluation and review

Marketing plans should be reviewed and should be measurable. Ensure that reviews and methods of measurement are planned from the outset and that all those involved understand what is being evaluated and in what timescale. For example, quarterly reviews may be helpful in keeping plans on track and relevant to changing business conditions.

Whose job is marketing?

The size of the business will dictate the marketing structure that is put in place. There are volumes of research (for example, *Marketing in SMEs*, by Simpson, Padmore and Taylor, May 2005) demonstrating that businesses, particularly those in the small to medium-sized category (most architectural practices), enjoy increased turnover and profitability if they have a specific and discrete marketing function and a structured approach to strategy and implementation.

It is important to secure buy-in from owners, partners and directors. Ideally, marketing needs a champion and advocate at a high level within the practice. Marketing activity needs to be well-documented, demonstrating the activity and results from the investment. Marketing can drive market knowledge and intelligence in the business to enable all those involved in working with clients and securing new business to be as effective and informed as possible.

SUMMARY

- Marketing strategy is about translating business plans, business objectives and aspirations into reality.
- The daily demands of a small practice and a lack of specific marketing expertise within the business need not create a barrier to formulating an effective marketing strategy.
- SWOT analysis is a useful tool to focus minds on the practice's current strengths. Review the practice's current position regularly and examine market trends and influences.
- PEST(LE) analysis is an efficient way of understanding changes in the market.
- Stakeholder mapping provides a measure of the key targets for communication.
- Ensure that everyone within the practice understands the marketing strategy and is motivated to deliver the practice's message.

Section 3
Business development: time to get hands-on

Roy Kent, *Kent Strategic Marketing Solutions*

It is important, even for the most established architectural brands, to realise that new business development is not so much about the present, but about the future. The business development decisions that the practice management team makes will influence the way the firm expands and provide a mechanism for survival in difficult times.

Business development

New business development involves breaking down barriers. These barriers differ according to the prospective organisation that is being targeted. Researching a market sector that the practice has strategically planned to break into will ensure that the leadership team in the firm is informed, allowing them to communicate more intelligently and effectively with clients in the quest to open the door to proposals and design initiatives and, perhaps more importantly, support moves to get any funding in place.

The very mention of the phrase 'business development' can send shivers down the creative spine. Hunting for new business makes many architects feel decidedly uncomfortable; but to ignore this vital element of marketing is perilous.

Business development is a strategic issue that requires a detailed tactical plan. It is a process that sets out to attract the attention of new clients and, in due course, to provide the practice with stimulating new design projects.

Essentially, planned business development comprises a set of pre-planned tactical actions that build a case for a client engaging one practice in preference to another. At the beginning, the potential client often has limited or no prior knowledge of the practice and its achievements to date.

Architects looking to build new business relationships need to communicate using a raft of different 'packets' of intelligent, relevant information that, over time, will change a prospective client's view. Building knowledge of the practice can shift a targeted prospective client's perception from blind ignorance to the possibility of a relationship that will be of mutual benefit.

Business development should be seen as a seamless extension of the marketing process, not as something operating in isolation from the design-led activities.

Plan for growth

A major concern for the senior managers of any business is the problem of growing too rapidly.

This should not be a concern for a well-organised architectural practice that has a strategic plan. The strategic plan is the blueprint for the way forward for any architectural practice. The plan should state the strengths and weaknesses of the current organisation, and provide an agenda for the management of change.

"The objective of planning for growth is to reduce risk."

The objective of planning for growth is to reduce risk. Of course, risk can take many forms. In the broader context, risk can relate to the economy. A buoyant economy with reasonable interest rates attached to loans is a conduit for expansion. If the economy's tectonic plates shift, for any reason, then confidence is shaken.

In relation to business development, this translates to a simple expedient – namely that the practice should remain focused on the strategic. Do not alter the course of the firm unless it becomes clear that it is simply foolhardy to carry on regardless.

When an economic downturn looms on the horizon, should the practice continue to seek projects from 'cutting-edge' developers or seek the comparative safety of government-funded schemes?

The answer is both 'yes' and 'no'. Yes, continue building the practice on its strengths in the sectors where it has a track record. And no, do not remain in a silo, exclusively dedicated to any one sector, no matter how robust that sector may seem.

Never allow all the practice's workload to remain in the hands of just one or two clients. As a rule, no single client should provide more than 40 per cent of fee income:

- projects should be sourced from a range of clients
- the workload of the practice must not be confined to any one sector, no matter how large or dynamic that sector is
- never rely on just one person within the practice to maintain contact with existing and prospective clients. What if that person leaves the firm, taking that client relationship with them?

Development of new business is not something to drift in and out of as time permits. It should be viewed as a day-to-day activity, carried out with focus and dedication to an agreed agenda.

Whatever the marketplace, it is important to be aware of how the client is going to view the firm. Capability statements, presentations and even informal conversations must all be alert to perception barriers, carrying strong messages to overcome any preconceptions.

Client preconceptions: barriers to winning new business

- 'Never heard of the practice'
- 'The practice is too small to be able to handle/resource the proposed project'
- 'The practice is too large to want to work on this small but boutique project'
- 'The practice does not have sufficient experience to be able to deliver the proposed project'
- 'The practice does not have sufficient expertise in sustainable design'
- 'We need a project architect who speaks Russian'

Assemble a team dedicated to business and client development

Every practice needs a business development team, even if it is just one person. If the practice consists of more than ten people, more than one person needs to be involved in new business development.

It is a moot point as to who is the right person to lead the business development team. If a senior partner decides to take up the role it should be on the basis of ability and not because of their years in the design sector. The team leader needs to be a facilitator, someone who recognises the skills of others and sets out to develop those skills for the benefit of both the practice and the individuals.

The team will function best as a blend of personalities. Alongside the architectural and design visionaries, the team must include someone with skills in graphic design who understands the power of images, and someone able to translate creative thinking into accessible, client-facing written text.

Background information on prospective clients

Once the decision has been made about which clients or market sectors are to be targeted, obtaining market sector and targeted organisation information that will intelligently inform business development decisions is vital. To obtain a profile of a particular company or government organisation, visit the prospective client organisation's website. Some websites do not provide the names of the individual directors. This is particularly true of the smaller property developers. This is a barrier, and can be very frustrating.

It is possible to get hold of this essential information, where quoted companies are concerned, by examining the online annual report uploaded to the company website. This will give the names of the board of directors.

Establish if a prospective client company is financially viable through a financial report ordered from the website of Companies House. The research can be very helpful in establishing confidence in the prospective client organisation, but it is

---

Companies House

The main functions of Companies House (www.companieshouse.gov.uk) are to:

1   incorporate and dissolve limited companies
2   examine and store company information delivered under the Companies Acts and related legislation
3   make company information available to the public.

important to remember that information filed at Companies House is historical. This means that the data filed may not reflect or be a good indication of the prospective client's current financial position. Analysis of the information discovered can provide vital intelligence. If, for example, the researched firm has yet to file accounts for the previous financial year, this may help decision-making on the organisation's financial viability.

Sector database

A database is simply a collection of information stored in a way that can be easily accessed and updated. Practices can use a database approach to build an intelligence resource concerning the clients and sectors that are being targeted. There are a number of ways to build a market-sector database. Some firms purchase listings of companies operating in a particular market sector. This information is usually supplied as a CD-ROM with the names of the senior decision-makers and full contact details that can be easily transferred to the practice's own prospect database.

With all commercial listing databases it is important to purchase the latest version. Check when the database was last updated when placing an order. Working from an out-of-date database could see an unacceptable percentage of postal returns on a mail shot and introduction emails found to be undeliverable.

Capture the data in a software program that suits the purpose. There are many options to chose from. Excel (at the simplest level and at a low cost as it is available as part of the Microsoft Office suite) spreadsheets can be fine tuned to exact requirements. Sage, from the accountancy software people, can be used to run databases very efficiently. ACT! is a customer relationship management tool that can be adapted to needs and logs data. Whatever the software platform used, just one person should be responsible for the integrity of the data, and for keeping the details held on the database up to date.

Market research

Market research is an important tool within the business development toolbox. It will give principals the confidence to know that effort, time and money spent to launch the practice into a new market, or build presence in an

---

How to glean information from recruitment ads

It always pays dividends to consult the quality newspapers, in particular the *Financial Times* (FT), *The Guardian*, *The Times*, *The Independent* and the *Daily Telegraph*. Be selective, and save time and money by scanning these newspapers online. The FT produces daily email notifications according to market sectors. Subscribing to these feeds can keep practice business development teams informed on areas of expressed interest and so can be incredibly useful.

The Guardian has a good reputation in the education sector, and has worked hard over the years to provide recruitment advertisements in this area. By scanning these ads once a week it is possible to find a nugget or two, and the names and addresses of key people in the field. For instance, the practice may be planning to target the estate managers/directors of UK universities. Individual websites may offer this information. It is often the case that when new personnel are required, these positions are advertised. Such advertisements may provide two pieces of intelligence: the prospective organisation may be expanding that department to cope with a new programme of work, or perhaps the old guard is retiring to make way for the new.

This, of course, is all supposition, but it does provide an opportunity to record the information on the practice database and to make contact with the new person appointed to the job when the vacancy has been filled.

---

existing sector, will be justified because there is enough potential work out there to make the initiative worthwhile. The type and size of any market research programme undertaken depends on how important the outcome will be to the practice and on the amount of investment and level of human resource that will be committed to delivering the market research project as a whole.

Market research is a systematic means of collecting the data and information relevant to a particular market sector that are needed to pave the way in an

---

Market research terms

Primary market research describes the direct collection of data from an informed respondent.

Secondary market research is more commonly known as desk research.

Quantitative market research is numerically orientated and requires the measurement of market phenomena. The information obtained is subjected to statistical analysis. Research can be collected in a variety of ways, including individual questionnaires or via the web, email and telephone.

Qualitative market research is far more subjective, based on the premise of how or why things are as they are at present. This type of research is usually gathered though 'face-to-face' meetings or arranged focus groups.

---

objective manner. Data collected can embrace the size and shape of the sector, the competition and even provide a 'guesstimate' of sector value.

The Building Centre

The Building Centre is an independent and established forum dedicated to providing information and inspiration across all sectors of the built environment. The Research Division provides UK and international clients with a comprehensive construction industry market research and information service comprising:

- full market appraisals, sector analyses, forecasts, competitor intelligence and market entry advice, distributor search services and ongoing marketing consultancy
- exclusive sector-specific market reports including contacts and decision-makers, as follows:
  - housing market intelligence reports
  - key housebuilder contacts
  - senior buyers in major contractors
  - key contacts in local authorities
  - key contacts in housing associations.

The Building Centre can also provide a mailing fulfilment service to many categories of contacts in the industry (www.buildingcentre.co.uk).

Other lists

The UK Commercial Developers Directory, available from Property Data for around £350, is a CD-ROM that contains the details of 1500 active commercial and mixed-use developers (www.propertydata.com). The comprehensive information provides the names and addresses of senior management and a financial snapshot of the top 350 companies.

Within the education sector, independent schools can be traced using the website of the Independent Schools Council (www.isc.co.uk). Although it is time consuming, visiting the website of each of these schools is invaluable. The larger schools will have in place a bursar or even an estates manager who should be the main contact on your database.

Routes to winning work

As well as generating work though active marketing within a sector, practices can generate opportunities through a number of more direct leads, all of which are discussed in Section 4.

SUMMARY

- Plan for growth – develop a strategic plan to manage change.
- Spread the practice's workload across targeted sectors. Avoid too narrow a focus on any given sector, no matter how dynamic.
- Plan for work from a number of clients – no single client should provide more than 40 per cent of the practice's fee income.
- Delegate the responsibility of winning new business to a business development team within the practice.
- Share the responsibility of looking after client relationships across the practice.
- Undertake client research, gathering background information on prospective clients.
- Understand the markets in which the practice wants to operate, collecting data on the dynamics of each market, the competition already present and a rough estimate of sector value.

Section 4
Bid management

David Grossmann, *Basler & Hofman*, and Helen Elias, *AECOM*

An architectural practice needs to manage the way in which it chases new business opportunities. Leaving things to chance is not going to win the practice the work that it would really like to be doing, let alone the clients for whom the senior staff aspire to be working. Like many other things in business, the key to success in managing new business bids and steering winning work in the direction that the firm really wants to be pursuing lies in the detail. This section explores the intricacies of bid development.

The process of winning architectural work starts with strategically considering new leads or opportunities, and then moves forwards along a structured journey towards the desired end. A structured bid process is needed, whatever the size of practice – and the principles behind developing the process remain fundamentally the same whatever the size or geographical reach of the firm. There is a perception that putting together an effective bid can absorb valuable time which could otherwise be devoted to creative design work and fee earning. All that is necessary is for the process to be adjusted according to the size and complexity of the business.

Preparing a bid document will be a lot easier if the principals in the firm have made some clear and direct decisions about the culture, aspirations and values of the business.

See also:
Section 1,
Marketing,
page 1

The strategic aim for managed bid development is to achieve consistency and cohesion in the structure and content of all submission documents and presentations being prepared within the practice. Without this joined up way of thinking and doing, the opportunity for chaos in the development of bid documents lies wide open.

Points to consider include the following:

- identify leads
- pre-bid discussions
- bid/no bid – the decision
- bid management
- proposal preparation and production
- presentation/negotiation
- measurement, review and feedback.

Identify leads

New architecture business opportunities can come through the door in a number of different ways. Frequent routes to a new business lead, however, can be via existing professional relationships, or through the official structured processes that have been put in place to advertise the need for a design team for publicly announced projects, such as OJEU.

The earlier in the process that the practice can find out about a project opportunity, the better. Multidisciplinary and multi-office firms should consider setting up a central clearing house system to coordinate all leads. An effective lead management process will save time and cost in the long run. It will also avoid the possibility of missing the opportunity to inform the person in the practice best placed to head up a bid for a potentially important project if the proposal is passed around in an ad hoc fashion until someone expresses an interest in picking it up. For these reasons, centralising the bid management process within the office or, for a multi-office practice, within one central business development team makes sense.

A recorded, managed system will ensure that bids are not submitted to single-entry opportunities from more than one team within the practice. An inadvertent double entry could result in both entries being rendered ineligible. Not only will this mean that a lot of time and effort has been wasted by all team members, but it could also affect relationships with those potential partners and influence their opinion of the practice as a viable partner for future

*See also:
Section 3,
Business
development,
page 39*

opportunities. If possible, arrange for the process to be coordinated by the same person or team. Handling lead opportunities requires an in-depth knowledge of the practice, the skills base available and the target sectors to which the firm aspires. More thoughts on how to identify leads are given in Section 3. The most common routes for finding leads are detailed below.

OJEU – the Official Journal of the European Union

All procurement in the public sector in the UK is subject to EU Treaty principles of non-discrimination, equal treatment and transparency. This means that under the EC Public Procurement Directives, for all public sector procurement, regardless of the size or nature of the project, the contracting authorities have to provide details of the procurements needed in a prescribed format. These opportunities to tender are published in the OJEU. European legislation currently dictates that supply and service procurements that are valued above a certain financial threshold must be advertised in the OJEU. Details of the thresholds can be found on the OJEU's website (www.ojeu.eu/Threshholds.aspx).

The transparency of this process means that all design firms that want to bid to be appointed as architects to a project advertised through the OJEU start from an equal position, with the same amount of information to take into account when putting a bid together. All architecture practices therefore have an equal opportunity to present their credentials and be considered for the project.

OJEU architecture advertisements can be found easily on the internet. They are published every day on the website Tenders Electronic Daily (TED – http://ted.europa.eu). This is the online version of the tenders supplement to the OJEU. It is the place to look for all new OJEU calls for tenders, contract awards and pre-information notices. It is best practice to assign a search of the site on a daily or weekly basis to a member of the business development staff, depending on the size of the firm and the time available to research business leads for work in the pubic sector. Busy organisations or firms that are unable to commit a staff member to this process, which can be quite time consuming, may choose to appoint an agency to perform this initial sift on their behalf. There are many agencies offering TED search services, delivering alerts on projects that meet specific identified search criteria.

Some bid invitations stipulate that one submission only will be accepted from any one firm expressing interest in the project. Check the bid criteria carefully to see if this is indeed the position. If this is the case, it will be important to manage the process of deciding which design team to align the firm with, or which engineers or other consultants to approach to form a joint bid.

Architectural competitions

Many high-profile projects in the UK will be the subject of an architectural competition. Competitions are a route for the client either to find the best architect to work on a project, or to see a raft of design solutions for a project, which will then lead to the appointment of an architect and design team. The rules of architectural competitions will vary from project to project, so it is worth checking the small print regarding what will be expected from the individual designer or collaborative team before starting work.

The main filter for many important architectural competitions in the UK is the RIBA. The RIBA has a dedicated team that works exclusively to help clients decide on the best form of competition for their project, and then manages the competition on the client's behalf.

More information about RIBA competitions and the competitions process can be found at www.architecture.com/competitions/

Types of competition

The format of an architectural competition is determined by the requirements of the client and the specific project. Each competition is tailored to individual client needs. Where there is a requirement for a client to comply with public sector procurement legislation (OJEU), then a competition has to be organised accordingly.

Standard competitive processes

There are a number of tried and tested competitive processes which enable a client to select either the right architect or design team for a project or the most appropriate design solution for a project:

- *Competitive interview to find the right architect* – Expressions of interest are requested from registered architects, with a shortlist being selected for interview. Only a broad project brief is required, and a commitment to build. Clients very often combine the competitive interview format with an invitation to prepare a limited amount of design work in response to a very general brief. Few 'pure' competitive interviews take place.

- *Open ideas competition* – To identify a range of possible design solutions, against a broad conceptual brief, with no commitment to build. Ideas competitions can be, and often are, open to students.
- *Open project competition to find a design solution* – Often a two-stage process, open to all registered architects, and with a detailed project brief and a commitment to build. Stage one involves anonymous submissions in response to the project brief. Anonymity is lifted in stage two, which usually involves between four and six teams and can require further design work and/or attendance at a final interview to present design ideas to a jury panel.
- *Invited competition to find a design solution* – Restricted to selected architects, with a detailed project brief and a commitment to build. Usually, six teams would be invited to take part. The firms to be invited can be selected in a number of ways: they may already be known to the client; the client may approach the RIBA Client Services for a shortlist; or, as happens in the majority of cases, the project may be advertised in the press and practices invited to submit details about their relevant experience.

Tailor-made competitions

The beauty of the competitive process is that it is completely flexible and can be adapted to meet the specific requirements of each client, and each project. Many clients choose to combine the design competition with the competitive interview. By introducing an interview element into the design process, the client is able to determine the likely working relationship with the competing design teams. Adapting the competitive process to the needs of individual clients is a skill that is intrinsic in the service offered by the RIBA Competitions Office.

RIBA Approved Competitions

An RIBA Approved Competition indicates to contestants that the Institute is involved in the management of the competition and that the competitive process conforms to best practice standards. Only competitions which are approved by the Institute can be associated with the RIBA name and logo.

To find out more about the RIBA competitions process please request a copy of the Guidance Notes for Clients via the RIBA Competitions website: www.architecture.com/competitions/

Invitations

Knowledgeable clients with a degree of understanding of the building procurement process may invite architects known to them to develop a proposal or presentation in response to a brief about a new project. Getting to know the key players in target market sectors through networking and relationship building is crucial for the practice to be able to take advantage of this route to new business.

Bringing work opportunities to prospective strategic partners by inviting them to join in a bid for a potential project is a good way of cementing business relationships for consultancy firms cross all design and technical disciplines. Any firm will look kindly on a practice that has presented it with an opportunity to bid for a significant project, potentially winning both organisations valuable work. Practices from all design and construction disciplines will be searching for new routes to business. Knowing the right people to call on, in order to put together the most appropriate team for an opportunity, is the key to gaining an invitation for the practice to join a team pursuing a particular opportunity.

When putting together a bid, approach firms that have similar cultural values and complementary design skills to allow the resulting team to be as rounded and appropriate to the project as possible. The earlier this process of exploring availability and interest in the project with potential strategic partners can begin, the better. Working ahead of the rest of the pack that is also chasing the same work will increase the chances of securing the partners that will work most effectively as a team.

If the bid calls for a united approach, then architects must be prepared to collaborate with other design firms to create a uniform team document. Sharing information across design teams and businesses will allow generic and individual bids, and the more run-of-the-mill formulaic bids, to carry the same messages, tone and values.

Development plans of organisations and institutions

Monitoring prospective client organisations and institutions in target sectors will alert the practice business development team to potential projects as they come to light. Following this route involves watching all target organisations closely to keep abreast of developments in order to be able to react immediately when a potential new project is being considered or is announced. Build contacts on the inside of the targeted organisations, promoting prior knowledge of the practice and its design abilities, to ensure that the firm is well placed in the event of an opportunity arising. Knowing people on the inside is a useful way to gain intelligence about potential opportunities ahead of the rest of the field.

Client contact and referrals

It is generally accepted in business that up to 80 per cent of most organisations' work comes as repeat business. The built environment is no exception to this rule of thumb. Keep in regular contact with past clients as they will very possibly be a source of future commissions. Current and past clients that are pleased with the work of their architects will frequently recommend their design team to colleagues and contacts within their own industry. Keep clients informed about the work of the firm – current projects, new services, key appointments and any new geographical capability in the UK or overseas.

RIBA Client Services

RIBA Client Services runs a dedicated client-driven referral service which produces a tailored shortlist of appropriate RIBA Chartered Practices, based on project information and specialisms supplied by them. These details are also used to support an online directory entry as well as produce sector-specific reviews which are sent out to a dedicated client database.

The team are also responsible for bridging the gap between RIBA members and clients – to communicate the value of good design and the advantages of good architecture and architects to clients. In addition, they support the RIBA Membership Services and Marketing team with ideas and client feedback to architects.

Further information on RIBA Client Services is available at www.architecture.com/useanarchitect, or email cs@inst.riba.org.

Website enquiries

Websites are the first place that any interested client prospecting for an architect will look. Make sure that clear contact information is given on the website and ensure that someone in the practice is briefed to respond immediately to any query that may come through from a new contact via the website. Some prospective clients may call the number of a contact name given on the website. Others may send in a query by email. Response tactics to an email query can range from a telephone call to replying electronically with a PDF practice brochure or capability statement. Whatever the methodology chosen, ensure that response to the initial query is immediate, then follow up the response with a call to see how the inquirer feels about taking matters further.

Recording ad hoc queries generated via the firm's website is one way of measuring how successful the marketing efforts of the practice have been. Log all queries, action taken and the outcome in order to build a picture over time of the nature of inquiry that the website is generating for the practice. Analysis of this information should be fed back in order to help steer the content, not just of the website, but of the firm's marketing strategy.

Prospecting for leads/cold calling

Cold calling is a hard way to win new business for a professional service practice operating in the intensely people-driven, highly networked architectural market-place. Calling out of the blue to introduce a firm is an approach that sits more comfortably within the product–supplier relationship than with a firm offering a professional, high-end design service.

Be prepared for a lot of negative response. Client organisations will frequently already have a cluster of consultant firms that they use on a regular basis, with whom they have established good relationships. Cold calling is very time consuming – it can take up to ten calls to get through to the targeted decision-maker, who, not having asked to be approached, could be, at the least, slightly resistant to receiving a pitch out of the blue and with no referring third party.

In addition to being time consuming, cold calling is tough – no one can take rejection for long without becoming despondent about the process. The fact that the practice is cold calling will probably not do its reputation any good either, once word gets around industry networks. In a relationship-driven industry such as construction, people tend to buy services from individuals whom they trust and firms that they know. There are better routes to obtaining the introductions that the firm needs than making cold calls.

Pre-bid discussions

All firms have their own individual ways of generating work. In the early years of a practice, a frequent philosophy can be to grab any project opportunity that comes through the door. However, as the firm grows, or as business becomes more successful, strategic criteria will be needed to help manage the work-winning process. Working strategically from the early start-up days will filter projects to allow the design teams to concentrate on winning work in market sectors that they especially want to cultivate.

The strategic criteria used by practices for selecting projects will vary from firm to firm. However, the points that are considered when choosing whether or not to invest time and resources in chasing an opportunity will usually include:

- brand
- knowledge
- reward
- market position
- employee attractiveness.

Questions to be asked that will guide the decision-making process about whether or not to move forward on an opportunity are set out in the box below.

Project selection criteria

Strategy – does the project market sector fit the company's long-term business strategy?

Desired outcome – what does the client want to achieve with this project: financial gain, reputation, environmental image, provision of high-quality space? Can the practice help this client to become more successful by providing the right building?

Experience – does the practice have a track record in this area gained by working on similar projects?

Client – does the practice want to work for this client? Is enough in-house knowledge available about this client's particular business sector to be able to demonstrate an understanding of their particular needs? Is the client financially sound? Will the practice be paid? Do we know anyone who has worked for this client before?

Location – where is the project to be built? Will it need to be designed by a team local to the site or can it be designed from elsewhere in the UK? If overseas, what local laws and design standards must be applied to the build? Will the practice need to work with a local partner to deliver the project to site?

Task – is the brief for what is needed from the consultant well-defined or vague? Can the practice really meet this brief? Can the team generate some initial ideas for how to respond to the brief?

Skills – has the practice got all the skills needed to do the job? Are these skills strong enough? Will the practice need to bring in contract staff or a sub-consultant or establish a partnering arrangement to round out the project team?

Risks – what are the risks associated with the project. Are the risks high or low? How much of a risk is the practice prepared to take?

Reward – are the potential rewards high enough for the project to be financially viable?

Staff – does the practice have the right staff (and technical resources) available to lead and deliver the project?

Price – will the client be looking for a quality, innovative design solution, or just the cheapest way to get the job done?

Partners – if the practice needs to unite with another firm to win the work, which possible partner will increase the likelihood of winning the bid? Has the practice worked with the potential partner firm before?

Competitors – who are the competitor practices that will also be pitching for the appointment? What is known of their tactics – are they likely to submit a realistically priced or an extremely low fee bid, for example? Against this field, does the practice stand a realistic chance of winning the work?

Intelligence – if there is not enough information to make an informed decision about whether or not to go for the opportunity, who in the practice is going to research additional information so that an intelligent decision can be made?

Invitation – it is unwise to commit the practice to accepting an invitation to join a design team without thinking carefully about the project first. Is this the best team for the practice to be associated with? Are other teams being pulled together that may stand a better chance of securing the appointment? Are there any background politics dictating that the practice might need to accept an invitation in order not to upset an existing professional relationship?

Exclusivity – for larger practices, the issue of exclusivity is very important. Entering a bid for a key project where the 'one bid per firm' rule applies means that firms may find themselves considering offers to align with one or two different design teams being pulled together to respond to the brief. Situations like this have to be dealt with by a very clear and strict process in order not to upset relationships, and team offers that are not attractive need to be declined gently.

Bid/no bid decision

Considering the project opportunity strategically, taking into account all the issues generated when asking the questions outlined in the box above, will help decision-makers to reach a position about whether or not it makes sense to push forward with the opportunity. It is as important to be able to decide not to follow up an opportunity as it is to be able to commit to developing a bid. Even in the largest of architect firms, available resources for researching the necessary issues and generating submissions will be limited. The most realistic route to achieving a high success rate on submissions is to make the strategic decision to follow up only those opportunities that align with the practice's long-term business strategy and where there is a strong feeling that the project is one that the practice stands a good chance of winning.

Sometimes the perception of a person who really wants to win a particular project may be biased. Build into the decision-making process a review of the bid/no bid decision with an independent person, as a check and balance. In some organisations, a points system is used in the selection process to achieve an unbiased result, but it is more important to ask the right questions and invest some time in finding out enough background detail than it is to debate endlessly about how many points to allocate.

Bid management

As a result of strategic decision-making, if the opportunity in question gets the go-ahead, then it is important to act on that decision as soon as possible in order to have all the necessary components in place by the deadline date.

The first step in the process is to bring together the right bid preparation team to work on the bid itself. The team should be led by a bid manager responsible for delivering the bid on time, to an acceptably high quality and within any allocated budget. The bid manager should be supported by a bid production team that is able to bring the whole initiative together as professionally as possible.

Confirm the team members as soon as possible, both internally and externally. Speak with any partnering firms joining in on the bid to establish contact with the people who will deliver the right images, information and other materials.

Proposal preparation and production

Producing a professional-standard bid document is a time-consuming process. Be realistic and ensure that there is enough time to pull the submission document together. Points to consider are detailed below.

Content

Be confident about the content of the bid document. Specific input relating to the project will need to be gathered from all relevant internal staff and external consultants involved. Workshops may be needed in which all the relevant personnel are invited to brainstorm ideas and share input into the outline creative solution that is to be proposed.

Standard information about practices, including generic capability statements, CVs and background information, always forms part of a submission. It is important to customise standard information to the bid. Make the bid document as specific and relevant, but short, as possible. Clients may lose interest if they have to read through too much irrelevant information. If external firms are involved, the firm putting the bid together will need to pull in the necessary information from the consultants in time to rework it into the correct format for the document in terms of layout and style.

Communication within the bid team

Establish a procedure for sharing information around the bid team to ensure that draft documents are passed to key people for approval, that information is generated and supplied on time and that all documents are supplied using the correct software platform.

Production

The actual production of a bid document from material generated by the team leader is often carried out under pressure, usually with a looming deadline driving the activity. Having a professional bid production team, if a larger firm, or at least one dedicated business development coordinator/administrator, will help the process enormously. Firms which rely on technical professionals to pull bid documents together need to be just as rigorous in making sure the right processes are in place to ensure not just consistency in the bids created, but accuracy in terms of content as well.

Efficiency can be greatly enhanced by making generic decisions about the bid production process.

The bid production process

Organise the information
Make the layouts available from one business development folder on the practice server. Duplicate the folder around each office if necessary. Ensure that each time the information in this folder is updated, previous pages are archived or removed to prevent out-of-date layouts or information finding their way into a document.

Page templates
Agree the design of a range of template formats for different page layouts. A flexible raft of page design options will avoid the situation where time-pressured staff are having to design the document as they go along.

Corporate information
Identify the chunks of information that are frequently requested and write generic statements about the firm in advance so that they can be grabbed, edited to suit the submission and flowed into the document. Scan all necessary certificates, ready for immediate use. A procedure will be needed to ensure the corporate information is kept up to date.

Project information
Maintaining a bank of bite-sized chunks of information about projects that are frequently incorporated into submissions, held in the business development folders on the server, will allow fast selection of the right information for use time and time again. (Ensure that there is a process for updating this information on a regular basis so that it is always accurate.)

Images
Agree a set of images (copyright secured) that are saved in the practice image library at the correct size, so that they can quickly be grabbed and dropped into the document without any additional formatting.

CVs
Ensure that a carefully written CV for each person in the practice who is likely to be included in a new business initiative is available in the business development server. If possible, add a photograph as clients like to be able to put a face to a name during presentations. Establish a procedure to ensure that CVs are updated regularly. The process must also ensure that CVs from new staff appointed at a senior level are captured.

Presentation/negotiation

If the initial bid document is successful, then the design team will invariably be called to give a presentation about the practice, ways of working and relationships with other consultant members of the design team. The presentation must include relevant information about the firm in relation to the project in hand. Ensure that the main speakers are confident, able people with a strong grasp not only of the technical issues set out in the brief, but also of the client, the marketplace and any prevailing economic conditions or risks that might have an impact on the project. Clients like to meet the people who will actually do the work so, as well as senior partners or directors, ensure that project architects are represented at the presentation. Agree fee bid proposals with other external consultants in advance of the presentation. It is important to rehearse carefully and present a united front when making a presentation. Think through the possible questions which a client might ask and prepare answers. Present to an experienced staff member who has not been involved in the bid process as if to the client – they will probably come up with the obvious questions that the client will ask.

A successful presentation may lead to an appointment in principle, which will then introduce conversations about fee levels. Discreet careful negotiations will eventually arrive at a point where all parties can move forwards with confidence. At this delicate stage in the process it is important to remain focused and realistic. Do not be tempted to drop fee levels to uneconomic levels in order to secure an appointment at any cost. The idea is to make money on the project, not subsidise the client in the delivery of their project, though there may be situations when one is 'buying' a project, for example to secure specific market or new sector entry or due to low work levels.

Measurement, review and feedback

Record all submission activity and log the results as the outcomes are announced. Winning submissions can be analysed for the successful features, which can then be shared around the business development department for roll-out in future bid situations. Feedback on a failed submission is usually available by phoning a named person to gather comments on the weak points as well as the good aspects of the bid. This feedback should be shared with the bid team as well, so that steps can be taken to improve on the critical points the next time around.

Analysing the number of submissions made over a year and monitoring success rates can provide useful key performance indicators for business development staff to work towards, as well as discussion points for staff personal development reviews.

In conclusion, a small practice with a team of fewer than ten people may well be able to put together bid documents in a more organic and less structured fashion than a major operation, which needs to take into account the separate ambitions of different offices and design teams, all clamouring to be included in a new business opportunity. Thus, it makes sense for a firm of any size to put a good bid management structure in place for researching business leads, making a decision on whether or not to go full tilt for the opportunity, and then deciding on how the bid document will look and what it will say. Closing off the entire process, being able to find out why the bid was either successful or unsuccessful will allow a form of measured feedback to be used, which will help to shape further bid documents as the practice moves forward.

SUMMARY

- Select new business leads and opportunities to follow up strategically, according to the practice's business plan.
- Engage in pre-bid discussions and establish project selection criteria to aid the process
- Establish a robust process for bid management, including developing appropriate and accurate content and presentation to a high standard.
- Create appropriate, engaging presentations. Rehearse all speakers and ensure that all team members attending the presentation are well-briefed.

Section 5
Branding an architectural practice

Michele Jannuzzi, *Jannuzzi Smith*

Architectural practices – large or small – are businesses that need to interact with their markets. An architectural practice that succeeds in developing a successful brand is a business with a clear advantage.

A logo, with its collateral graphical elements, is only one aspect of an architectural brand – the quality of a product, the reliability of a service, the people involved, the ever-expanding plethora of marketing activities and the way the firm is positioned within the market, all discussed in Sections 1 and 2, will contribute to the development and success of the brand.

Some of the fundamental principles for brand-building within the architectural sector are the same as those in any type and size of business, but there are specific attributes that apply solely to architects. This section considers some key aspects that anyone establishing a new practice or rebranding an existing architectural firm should consider.

The need for a strategy

As explained in Sections 1 and 2, marketing and communication strategies are essential for the long-term success of a practice. Similarly, a strategy is needed to carry forward the brand for the firm. The bigger the scale and wider the reach of the practice, the more difficult it becomes to tie together the many brand touchpoints of a busy architectural firm into one simple branding strategy that supports the firm's marketing and communication strategies.

A corporate identity is both a contributor to and a user of the brand strategy. As a contributor, the corporate identity of the practice proposes key (and lasting) visual solutions. As a user, a strategy is needed in order to develop the corporate identity in the first place. It is a 'chicken-and-egg' situation that is often resolved by developing the two simultaneously.

Choosing your brand or brochure designer

The most important aspect to bear in mind throughout the process of selecting a designer is that the person or agency is being appointed to help the practice. It is therefore paramount that the practice's business needs are thoroughly understood, and are communicated to the design firm as part of the brief, so that requirements can be matched to the design skills and expertise on offer.

A visual identity will accompany the business for many years, and thus will need to evolve over time. It is important to consider future flexibility of a brand identity when appointing a designer. Affordability, availability and proximity are all aspects that may be resolved within a three-month design project, but may cause all sort of issues throughout the subsequent years unless factored in from the beginning.

Be sure to indicate the budget that the business can sustain at the outset of the branding or design project. A professional brand designer will be able to advise

"Good design provides an asset for the business"

on how best to proceed and how to ensure that the money spent is turned into a sustainable investment that will contribute towards the firm returning a profit. Good design provides an asset for the business and should not be seen as a mere cost in the annual balance sheets.

Coming up with a shortlist

Drawing up a good shortlist requires substantial effort. Avoid precluding the development of a good corporate identity by making a rushed, badly informed five-minute decision. Consider designers or agencies already known to the practice. They are likely to know the business and be able to make a faster start on the project in hand.

The directories of professional bodies can assist in finding a new firm of graphic designers. The Design Council (www.designcouncil.org.uk) offers practical advice and a list of directories to consult. Look at recent winners and nominees of design awards. The most prestigious design awards in the UK are the D&AD Awards (www.dandad.org), but a number of institutions also run respectable competitions.

Architecture and design magazines can be a good place to pick up names and to get a feel for the pulse of what is currently going on. There are many good designers out there and not all of them are featured in magazines or compete in awards, so be sure not to preclude any design firm simply because it is not published or listed.

Last, but not least effective, is to ask contacts to suggest design firms.

Selecting your designer

Once a shortlist of potential design firms is drawn up, the next step is to evaluate the options. It is important to meet the people so you can ask questions on their approach and their past projects and establish whether or not a good working relationship could be developed with them.

Two methods are used to select a designer: a credentials pitch and a creative pitch. Unless the budget available for the design project has six figures or more of design business to award (or enough extra budget to fund it), avoid the creative competitive pitch route. No respectable design professional will invest ten days of creative work in a speculative pitch to win possibly just ten days of paid work. Consider, instead, asking shortlisted design firms to give a credentials pitch – presenting creative work pitched to and completed for other clients.

In-house versus outsourcing

Many architects have a business case for resourcing graphic design internally, generally for assisting the presentation of architectural project submissions and reporting documents.

The ultimate goal of a corporate identity is to raise the level of graphical presentation of a business – in this respect, to have an in-house person or team can only be seen as an advantage. It is, in fact, a great asset that will afford the practice a more comprehensive implementation and could allow for a more challenging corporate identity.

However, possessing in-house graphic design skills does not automatically mean that the expertise is available in-house to tackle the corporate identity development project. The design staff will have their hands full doing what they have been employed to do, and they may not have the specific experience to contribute to a full rebrand. If the in-house team has the potential, include them in the shortlist and evaluate their expertise and skills against the rest of the shortlist.

The corporate identity

The glossary of possible terms and headings in marketing and communication strategies is extensive: brand audit, brand commitment, brand earnings, brand essence, brand experience, brand mission, brand platform and brand vision are just a few. Avoid the jargon and keep it simple. To inform the development of a corporate identity for the practice, give some answers to a few basic questions:

- What does (or should) the brand stand for?
- Who is the brand for?
- Where will it be used and seen?

Brand values and brand positioning

Brand values are a brief description of the firm's qualities. Brainstorming these qualities may lead to some trade-offs between reality and aspirations, but it is critical to identify credible values. Figure 5.1 presents an example of the different brand values of two competing airlines.

Brand values create a checklist against which it is possible to evaluate and direct all marketing activities for the practice, including, first and foremost, the development of visual elements, including the logo. There should be a distinct correlation between the brand values and the corresponding marque.

Brand positioning is the place that a brand occupies in the marketplace. Diagrams of all sorts are widely used as a way to pinpoint a brand's position relative to its competitors. This approach can be used to differentiate the brand of the practice from the rest of the architectural market.

A case for persona

Categorise audiences to assess who is at the receiving end of the different communication outputs generated by the practice. When developing a brand

FIGURE 5.1: *The brand values of EasyJet and British Airways reflect the culture and aspirations of each organisation*

EasyJet	British Airways
1. Great value	1. Safe and secure
2. Taking on the big boys	2. Professional
3. For the many not the few	3. Warm
4. Relentless innovation	4. Thoughtful
5. Keep it simple	5. Responsible
6. Entrepreneurial	6. British
7. Making a difference in people's lives	
8. Honest, open, caring and fun	
source: www.easy.com/values/index.html	source: http://www.britishairways.com/travel/british-airways-sponsorship/public/en_gb?gsLink=searchResults

– as with any product – a crowd of diverse target audiences is complex to embrace.

The problem that arises when considering a group of target audiences is the large number of potential constraints. Accommodating the differences within the audience group (sector, regional or technical audiences) can often result in a homogenised solution, an attempt at a one-size-fits-all response. In terms of a practice brochure and website, the result will almost certainly be unsatisfactory. It is hard to produce one item that meets the needs of a diverse range of target audiences.

Consider creating an ideal persona (or a limited number of personas) to encapsulate the probable audience instead of the possible audience (Figure 5.2). This will give focus to the design brief and, in consequence, to the solution.

Anticipate requirements

Brand building is a long-term affair, so it is paramount to ensure that whatever brand the practice develops is sustainable over time. The brand will need to work for key and long-term marketing activities. A list of likely implementations is an invaluable

FIGURE 5.2: *Diagram presenting the correlation between messages and personas for the marketing program of Central Saint Martins College of art and design*

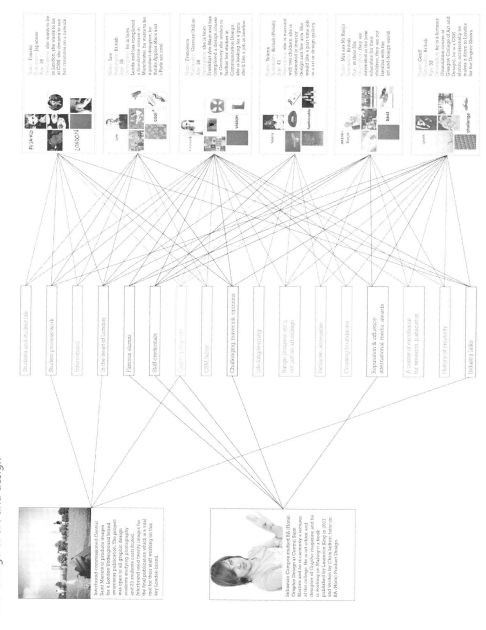

tool in assisting the development of a brand to ensure it has all the required delivery elements. In compiling the list, include the usual suspects, such as stationery and a sign on the door, as well as the obvious website and brochure applications.

Developing a corporate identity

Names matter because they are often the first item of communication a practice can get across. The golden rule of a successful name is 'short, pertinent and memorable'. IBM, Sony and Nike are all good examples.

When developing a brand name for a practice of architects, consider the volume of contacts and the penetration the practice wants to achieve in the market and trading sectors.

A first route to a practice name is often an acronym based on the name of the founding partners. However, acronyms rarely say anything meaningful about anyone or anything. Some form of 'power' is needed in order to impose a name on the marketplace – generally the type of power only within the grasp of large corporations. So, if the firm cannot sustain large marketing and public relations operations, ensure that the name does enough to set it apart and helps to say what the practice actually does.

Case study: rebrand and brand implementation

An architectural practice, which had recently renamed itself and rebranded, asked Jannuzzi Smith to come up with a concept for a small brochure. The main purpose of the brochure was to inform their existing clients about the name and brand change.

The project demanded a considerable amount of new effort, including the content development, design, production and distribution of the brochure. In discussions with the architects, Jannuzzi Smith uncovered a document (produced in Microsoft Word) that the practice sent to existing clients several times every month. By redesigning this document and ensuring that the rebrand was implemented successfully and the change communi-cated, the desired end result was achieved for the practice at a fraction of the cost of a full-on rebrand brochure.

When choosing a name it is important to consider what may happen to the business in the long run. Expansion is a likely outcome – with more people coming in as partners and wanting to add their name to the brand – and possible migration into different markets, languages and cultures.

Increasingly, the internet and, more specifically, search engines play an important role in how potential clients will find the practice. A name that translates well into a web address is also an advantage.

The logo

Without doubt, the logo is the undisputed king of corporate identities: it is the visual element that stands for someone's or something's name. The solution generally consists of a logotype or logogram, in some cases accompanied by an image: a symbol, a pictogram or any other type of illustration.

An architect's logo will be applied across applications of every size, from letterheads to site boards and exhibition stands, on paper and on screen in websites and digital applications and possibly even be etched onto the basement stones of buildings.

Case study: the brand name has to be practical

When our studio set up in business in 1993, the question of the name was one of the first to be raised. Of course, being graphic designers, it had to be a name that could be turned into a good logo. After long and extensive peregrinations we settled for the simplest of all: the only common letters in our two surnames (Jannuzzi and Smith) were 'ii'. It looked perfect: the two vertical lines headed by a roundel beautifully expressed our disposition towards minimalist design and brilliantly illustrated the nature of the partnership – a two-man band.

After days of pain and frustration the joy in our own branding decision was overwhelming . . . at least until we had to answer the phone and announce 'ii'. At the time, answering the phone with the practice's name was the only piece of marketing we could afford and the 'ii' clearly was not going to work as a verbal extension to our brand. The idea was irreversibly dropped. We then named our practice Jannuzzi Smith.

Thus, in order to decide on a logo it is critical to review where it is likely to end up being used, and what the firm wants the logo to achieve. The communication strategy and list of likely implementations of the brand will come in very handy for informing the decision. A single logo is not necessarily the only answer – there may be a need for more than one logo, or a logo that can be adapted to suit many different versions and applications, from print to web to digital communication outputs.

Brand architecture (a family of brands and sub-brands) may be needed to satisfy complex end-use requirements. Remember to take into account the consideration that managing a family of logos is more demanding than managing one logo.

Many aspects of marketing the practice will change to adapt to different market conditions, but the firm's visual signature is not likely change. A sensible brand manager will create a name and a logo that will serve the practice for as long as possible, and will try to predict the causes that could compel major changes.

Typefaces and typographic styles

Choosing a typeface or a selection of typefaces for all forms of communication, both printed and on screen, is a proven way to bring consistency to the graphical presentation of an architectural practice.

Architects have a preference for picking sans-serif faces – one assumes to better reflect the contemporary connotations of their work. There is a whole world of font shapes and styles to choose from. The chosen typeface will say a lot about the practice.

It is important that the typeface selected is able to do all that is required of it, and not just render a logotype. There is always the option of mixing-and-matching: to combine a font for the logo and, for instance, titles with a different family of fonts to be used for body text.

As a rule of thumb, do not go overboard and choose to work with too many typefaces. 'Less is more' works as a guiding principle in graphic design terms as well as in architecture. Also, licensing many fonts can become expensive.

Set a number of styles to run across the typographic matter for all communi-cation collateral produced by the practice.

The styles may encompass the following:

- set sizes for headings and text
- the use of italics, small capitals and bold
- conventions for punctuation (especially when it comes to the use of capital letters).

It is an extra task to implement (and police) the set style, but the typographic consistency achieved throughout all resultant marketing material adds to the professional presentation of materials produced by the practice. As the firm grows and perhaps establishes a number of design groups or offices, each producing its own documents, such a style guide will become crucial to maintain consistency across all outputs generated by the different design teams.

The internet today can be a limiting factor as only a few fonts are supported by most operating systems and most browsers. One alternative is to create bitmap images (JPG, GIF, PNG) to be displayed on-screen, but this is hardly a solution, as it makes long text cumbersome and inflexible. It is worth keeping an eye on this problem. Technology moves fast and it is just question of time before a workable solution will be found.

Colours

It is an established fact that a coordinated use of colour (deciding on just one colour or a palette of colours) results in a more recognisable graphical presentation for the practice. However, the proliferation of different media and marketing opportunities can present the brand manager with the problem of consistency.

There are several colour systems in use across different industries. For the printing industry the most widely used are:

- CMYK: a four-colour process of cyan, magenta, yellow and key (black), generally used to render photographic images
- Pantone: special mixes of inks to compound one single colour.

RGB (red, green and blue) and HexDec values are the established way to specify on-screen colour, and there are also numerous other systems corresponding to paints, varnishes and all types of materials.

The primary concern is colour management – to achieve a consistent colour performance across different monitors, printing processes, papers and other materials.

Professional brand designers will be able to advise on an appropriate solution. As with a family of logos and typefaces, the more adventurous the decision, the more time and effort will need to be invested in specifying and later implementing the selected palette of colours consistently across a range of media.

Images, and the use of images

Images make the work of the practice – completed buildings, competition entries and design details – apparent at a glance.

By the very nature of what they do, architects create some of their own copyright-free images using computers, 3D software and digital cameras. This means that a flood of material can be made available to develop marketing collateral, ranging from the website to project sheets and brochures. Business development managers will also need project images and technical drawings to populate pre-qualification documents and submission proposals.

To ensure that the images do some work for the practice brand, over and above the fulfilment of the architectural requirements, there are a few rules of which to be aware:

- *Be print aware* – always create images in a manner suitable for professional printing. Printed material requires images with a greater definition than an item that is to be desk-top published using conventional laser and inkjet printers or is for on-screen display only. Set up an organised image library to archive all image files and make sure that the resource is backed up so the original high-resolution image files are not lost. Once the definition of an image is lost it can never be recovered.
- *Image consistency* – promote a consistent and appropriate style and visual grammar to all images collected to populate the image library and to be used for marketing resources. Consistency in the style and standard of images will play an important part in conveying the essence of the firm's work, as well as making presentations across any print or digital platform look more professional. Some architects will commission only a limited number of photographers to capture their projects on completion, to assert a unique photographic language for how the practice presents its work.

A consistent approach to production of sketches, technical drawings, CAD renderings and other images produced and used by the practice in marketing activities and presentations will build over time into a comprehensive resource of images united by visual consistency. This will enable a continued and consistent visual language in the production of materials, ranging from brochures and project sheets through to submission documents, PowerPoint presentations and the practice website.

Make your images available

Storing images in an image library is a good idea. Set up a workable indexing system in order to be able to quickly search for and retrieve images. As they grow, image libraries can be complex to manage, especially when images include files of different sizes and copyright permission information (to ensure no image is used without the correct permissions).

Some firms develop a bespoke system for managing images and controlling the use of copyright-protected images. There are a number of off-the-shelf image library software packages available that can help a practice to manage its image library. An image management package enables organisations to manage, catalogue, share and automatically re-size images to insert into a range of documents, such as PowerPoint presentations or reports. Users are delivered images at the right size and resolution, saving time when producing bespoke submission materials.

Production: processes and materials

Non-standard materials and production processes are a great way to bring that extra edge to graphical presentations – especially when considering architecture's affinities with three-dimensional forms and materials.

Despite major developments in the print industry, current print habits still lean towards conventional full four-colour processes, printed on a coated paper stock. Printing is a centuries-old art that retains many of its secrets. Character can be added to the practice's printed communication materials by exploring the possibilities of combining inks, varnishes, materials, bindings and other processes – old or new.

As with photographers, it is useful to limit the number of printers and suppliers that the practice uses. Once all of the firm's specific print requirements have been assimilated, an appointed printer will be able to streamline management and production and, above all, guarantee consistency.

The tools

Every business is unique and a different set of tools is necessary to help an architectural practice achieve visual consistency in the design and production of materials. An important area to consider is the use of corporate identity manuals, which can be supported by standard templates and document libraries.

Manuals

Documentation of guidelines, practices and processes is good for any area of your business – and corporate identity is no exception. Large companies with complex structures or global operations spend significant sums of money devising detailed style manuals because they recognise the associated benefits of consistency across all outputs through compliance with the manual. Smaller companies can also take advantage of having a corporate identity manual. But be aware that a corporate identity manual is only useful if it is maintained and the output policed.

Establish the corporate identity manual as a set of principles and information to guide design and print processes and not as a long list of 'do not's, which would progressively leach any life from the brand.

A corporate identity manual should not be considered a *fait accompli*. It may start as little more than short descriptions of logotypes, colour and usable typefaces, but will inevitably integrate descriptions of good solutions and successful processes that provide useful information for future implementation.

The way forward for in-house document production: automated publishing systems

Computers have transformed the way we work. There is hardly anything that is designed and produced today that is not, at some point along its journey, managed by a processor. However, databases and digital asset management tools have not made quite the same impression on our daily working lives and have failed to bring order to the terabytes of data we produce around the clock.

Perhaps the day of the fully integrated publishing system, seamlessly interlinking different aspects of a business – from development to implementation and from archiving to marketing – is still a distant dream. Or perhaps not. Online digital applications are gradually taking over all sort of processes; intranets are turning into collaborative working environments; distribution of information is rapidly shifting from paper-based media to the internet.

For the average architectural practice, organised data management brings real advantages. Architects produce data and data is intellectual property. Over time, if the data is properly managed, it becomes an asset. The practice's marketing and communication functions can be the first beneficiaries of such an asset.

Introduce applications to aid the communication processes. Graphical elements (such as logos, typefaces and images) can be integrated with guidelines, styles and layout templates in a 'production engine', such as Microsoft SharePoint, where the resources are all processed together.

The benefits of database publishing are manifold and not only confined to the web. A cross-media publishing tool can produce highly detailed QuarkXPress or Adobe InDesign documents (for printing) as well PDF and HTML documents for websites – each optimised dynamically for their respective medium and quality of output.

The use of an automated data management tool gives the following key advantages:

- Design input can be contained in predetermined templates, empowering the user to create and recreate marketing materials such as project sheets, flyers, invitations, reports, submissions and standard documents, all on demand and all embracing the branding guidelines.
- The burden of repetitive, data-intensive and error-prone tasks is removed.
- Improved efficiency allows each piece to be produced more quickly and with less effort, significantly reducing costs, freeing resources and extending marketing periods significantly.
- Written content is inputted and managed independently from the design and production process, both for website and printed publications, creating a harmonious, collaborative working environment.

The creation and management of case studies and project descriptions is a recurrent headache for all architectural practices and presents the perfect opportunity to employ automated data management.

Marketing collateral: brochures and websites

When it comes to producing specific materials, it is essential to start by identifying exactly what the item under consideration is to be used for. Different end uses and audiences will dictate the quality and content of any piece of marketing collateral. Two things that regularly appear on the list of architectural practices' communication resources are brochures and a website. These two items will frequently be the main resources for the firm. Careful planning is essential so that the end results meet expectations and communicate the practice effectively to its audiences.

Brochures

The average time that a reader will devote to a printed brochure is around nine seconds. Printed collateral may not be read from cover to cover, but a successful, well-written, well-designed and well-produced brochure will quickly communicate the culture, ability and aspirations of the firm.

The format of a brochure can range from a simple folded sheet at A5, A4 or other size, to a complex, large document on which many hours of time and effort have been spent. Selecting the right solution results from analysis of audience, expected use of the end product, and available budget.

It is also important to develop a brochure as a product designed to a planned delivery method. Brochures can be handed out as a support tool at meetings. If they are to be posted, make sure the end result is robust enough to withstand being transported through the mail system. A brochure that is too heavy will rack up the postage costs, while a delicate item will need special packaging – again, an additional expense, as well as a potentially time-consuming extra task for busy staff.

Alternatively, it is becoming common practice to develop brochures for issue as a PDF document only, a sustainable way forward for issuing marketing communication tools. Be aware, however, that if the receiver of the PDF does not have a good quality printer, and chooses to save and print the document, it may not look as sharp as it does on the screen.

Some practices chose to develop a mix of printed and PDF brochure resources to build a range of marketing communication products.

Smaller architectural practices may get away with a single brochure to set out their stall. Strategically, it is rare to find a brochure for a medium to large sized firm which captures everything that the practice can offer and speaks to all audiences. The classic way to split brochure-driven information is through sets of sector-led, design discipline led or regionally led products.

Websites

Website design has to work quickly across a wide range of audiences, from the casual browser to the specific search. It is said that any website has about three seconds to engage and grab the attention. Designing a website is a sophisticated and increasingly complex process, which makes use of a framework based on digital code and display technology to build and keep up to date an online environment for information about the practice.

A website is not a product that can be created, launched and then left to fend for itself. Website maintenance and development is an ongoing activity – for many architectural practices this is the most important form of communication with audiences across all client sectors, as well as a key recruitment tool. It is therefore important to plan very carefully what the website is expected to do for the practice, and to develop a site that is affordable to deliver and easy to maintain in order to keep the content and images fresh.

A good rule of thumb is to try to keep the site as simple as possible, and to keep the hierarchy of the site flat. Too many levels in a site can make it complex to navigate around. The visitor should ideally not be able to move more than three clicks away from the home page.

"keep the site as simple as possible"

When developing a website, use the following process points to help guide decision-making and keep the project evolving logically:

- purpose of the website
- site structure plan
- hosting/domain name
- content management
- functionality and interaction options
- content development: written text, supporting images
- graphic design

- site development and coding
- testing
- website launch.

The technical side of website development is best left to the experts. Needless to say, key decisions that will need to be made at an early stage will include compatibility of the site with the different web browsers that are in popular use, and different image file formats. The only way to be certain that a new website will work on a given platform is to test it. Tips on how to develop written content for a website are given in Section 11. There are plenty of good books available that examine the subject of website design and development in more detail. It is advisable to consult an expert for advice on the most up-to-date systems and approaches to creating an online presence.

See also:
Section 11,
Writing skills
for marketing
collateral,
page 147

RIBA Microsites

The RIBA offers a specialist website development service, available at a discount to its chartered practices. *RIBA Microsite* is offered through the RIBA's partner Acefolio, and is an excellent low-cost opportunity to create a credible and effective web presence.

The key features of an RIBA Microsite:

- A flexible, self-edited practice website (microsite), with variable design options and both practice and RIBA branding across a maximum of eight fully editable sections, including: Portfolio, News, Focus, Jobs, Profile and Contacts. Absolutely no web development expertise is required.
- A secure RIBA-branded account area through which all marketing assets can be managed and published to the practice's RIBA Microsite, which can handle data, images, PDFs and even videos. Full training and support materials are provided.
- A fully branded digital brochure tool offering quick and simple RIBA-branded e-brochures.

Further information on *RIBA Microsite* is available at www.acefolio.com, or email riba@acefolio.com or call 05601 411 306.

Written content

Alongside brand identity and images, the third essential component of the development of any communication resource, from website to brochure, is the quality of the written content. Consistency of message, tone and voice across all outputs is essential in order to present a united suite of materials, whether in print or online. Writing for marketing collateral is addressed in detail in Section 11.

```
┌─────────────────┤ S U M M A R Y ├─────────────────┐
│                                                     │
│  • Marketing and communication strategies are essential for the long-term
│    success of a practice.
│  • A practice's visual identity is a long-term investment so the selection of
│    the brand designer must be handled with care.
│  • Brand values and positioning should be brainstormed to ensure that the
│    practice's ethos is clearly reflected.
│  • The practice name and logo are vital elements in establishing the brand
│    in the marketplace.
│  • Consistent graphical presentation across all forms of communication is
│    crucial.
│  • A well-maintained image library is an essential element in the presen-
│    tation of all the practice's visual material.
│  • Brochure and website design needs expert input to achieve maximum
│    impact.
│                                                     │
└─────────────────────────────────────────────────────┘
```

Section 6
Public relations

Helen Elias, *AECOM*

A successful practice needs to establish its reputation within a crowded marketplace, and then keep information flowing to clients, prospective clients and the industry at large. The public relations (PR) function looks after reputation, managing the way in which the practice communicates proactively with its audiences. This section touches upon the different ways in which an architectural practice can talk to the wider business community to develop, establish and protect its reputation and brand.

All architectural firms need to invest time in managing their brand and their reputation. Working in a silo, heads down and focusing exclusively on design, is not going to get the practice known in the marketplace, and is certainly not going to draw in the firm's next big project.

From the very start, every practice should consider its PR function from a business perspective. As discussed in previous sections, the firm will need a business plan and a marketing strategy. In turn, part of the marketing strategy should include a strategy for managing PR, communicating the work of the practice and engaging with the professional client and industry print and online media communities, using as many different methods and tactics as possible to get the message out there. The plan should also include the development of any marketing collateral that may be needed – from the website to printed brochures. All materials should be developed to reflect the brand of the practice.

See also: Section 5, Branding an architectural practice, page 65

PR strategy

It is important to plan the public-facing activities of any architectural practice. The plan should include how the firm will seek attention from, and engage with, all audiences, including the media.

The PR strategy should reflect and support the short-term and long-term business development aims and objectives of the practice. The strategy must be realistic, taking into account the resources that are available within the firm to ensure that the PR function keeps ticking over. This is an important job, and responsibility for who takes the lead on the firm's external communication function needs to be firmly established. Smaller firms should appoint a practice principal or senior member of staff to take the lead; medium-sized and larger practices may recruit a full-time PR professional, include PR skills in the job

See also: PR consultants, page 97

description for the practice's marketing member of staff or consider hiring a PR consultant to carry out the external communication function.

Things to consider when developing a PR strategy include:

- the firm's key messages and how the practice wants to be seen in the marketplace
- media relations
- what collateral is needed: website, brochures, bid documents
- budgets and resources.

Key messages

Consistency in tone and presentation of the practice over time is essential. One way to ensure that all promotional activity is consistent is to agree what the key messages of the practice are, and then ensure that these messages are reflected in all client-, market- and public-facing initiatives.

The key messages are the anchor points that appear consistently across all of the communication materials and outputs of the practice. They are vital ingredients which, through their repeated use, effectively build continuity that over time establishes the reputation of the brand. Key messages can sometimes be referred to as 'elevator statements'. These are a crisp, concise summary of the activities and culture of the practice – the kind of quick précis that can be delivered by clients and influencers who know the firm when they are describing it to someone else in the short time it takes for the lift to rise a few floors, or to friends gathered round the barbeque.

What are the key trading points of the practice on which its reputation is being built? The key messages should reflect the main points of expertise that the partners really want the firm to be known for, and also include visionary aspirations for the firm (for example, contemporary design, sustainability, good employers, reliable, traditional materials, technology, school design).

Taking time to establish these points is worth the effort. The key messages have a continuing influence internally across a practice, influencing staff recruitment and setting quality standards to which performance can be matched. Develop the messages with the practice's audiences firmly in mind.

Keep the key messages short and to the point. Use bullet points to define the messages. The messages should be memorable and truly represent what the practice does and aspires to do, capitalising on the unique selling points of the practice that make it stand out from its competitors. These are the words that the audience must absorb and associate with the practice, so they need to be carefully chosen. Once the key messages have been agreed upon, ensure that all staff are fully briefed – after all, these messages will inform and reflect the culture of the company now and in the future.

Media relations

Publicising the practice can happen organically, usually driven by media interest in high-profile or technically interesting projects. However, it is rarely the case that a young firm of architects will see the press beating a path to its door without alerts about key people, projects or other issues being drip-fed to journalists to raise awareness and interest.

The long-term PR strategy should set out to systematically educate identified target audiences about the practice though the medium of the press across all outputs – print, broadcast and online. Publicity and reputation building cannot be left to chance. Ad hoc appearances in the media will not keep the practice in the line of sight of the key industry people who need to be reminded about the firm's work and skill set. The practice's reputation will be better served by regular presence in the media throughout the year.

PR is always going to be an opportunistic activity, and there will doubtless be peaks and troughs in successfully getting the practice into the news. However, by strategically looking ahead to identify opportunities to generate publicity, there is a greater chance of the practice developing a consistent public profile, and not leaving the opportunity to talk to the media about a project until it is too late.

Generating publicity can be quite time consuming, and there is no guarantee that the effort put into publicising a project through the media will result in the desired press coverage. But there is more chance of PR activity being successful and generating column inches about the practice and its projects if the activity is planned and mapped out.

Consistency

Architects will, at times, work on projects that may be highly confidential, either at the start or all the way through the design process. An untoward comment to the press could result in a great deal of damage to the relationship between the practice, the client and other stakeholders in the project.

A sensible solution is for one person to act as coordinator for all press work on the project, with either management authority to speak on behalf of the practice or a clear line of contact to senior management for instant decision-making when an important press call comes along. Journalists who make contact with other members of staff should be referred to the media contact (usually known as the press officer).

Establish a process for dealing with the media to remove ambiguity about how the media relations function is handled across the practice. The result will be that the firm will be seen to be speaking with consistency to the media.

- Is one person/team responsible for dealing with calls from journalists or is the project partner/leader the best person to put a press query through to?
- Does the senior management or one appointed top person need to be consulted about every comment that is made to the media?
- What happens if journalists talk to other members of staff?
- Who in the practice is authorised to speak to the press?
- Who is the member of staff designated to handle media enquiries? Is this person authorised to act as company spokesperson?

Include the ground rules in any office procedure/intranet and new staff induction pack.

Coordinated approach

Reasons for a coordinated approach to handling press relations include:

- ensuring approved information is issued to the media
- ensuring no press embargo is being broken
- ensuring no contractual confidentiality clause is being broken
- ensuring the information being issued is timely
- central handling of a problem that the press has got wind of
- information being issued as part of a planned campaign
- consistency of information issued
- accuracy of information issued
- consistent issuing of key messages about the practice
- ensuring there is client and stakeholder approval for media activity.

Appointing one person to be the contact for the media gives journalists a name to get to know. Journalists are busy people with deadlines to meet, so handling a media query by providing accurate, approved information quickly, or clearing the way for the journalist to speak to the most appropriate person without having to make numerous time-consuming calls to different people, will increase the chances of their coming back to the practice on other occasions.

Champions and experts

It will help the press officer considerably if the practice leadership team prepares a list of experts with the mandate to speak on specific issues that align with the company's interests and skill set. The press officer can thus check material with the expert or pass the journalist to the design discipline or sector expert or project spokesperson for interview rather than having to try to be knowledgeable about all subject areas, projects and design disciplines.

Media training

If the experts or spokespeople nominated to speak on behalf of the practice are nervous about talking to journalists, and it looks as if there might be a run of press interest on a project or issue that will prompt media interviews, consider sending the appropriate people on a media training course so that they are briefed on how to speak to journalists. It can

See also: Talking to the press, page 96

be a pleasure to talk to journalists about the design specifics of a project for a building study or technical feature. However, giving a media interview on a sensitive topic is not such a straightforward thing to do. It is easy to say the wrong thing or let slip some information that should not be in the public domain. If possible, in advance of a press interview that could be tricky, jot down the key points or check with the client to see if there is a particular line to take on an issue.

Target audiences

Issuing information to the press about the practice or a project will be more effective if the material is targeted at specific audiences, and the content of press releases developed accordingly.

Target audiences for architects usually include:

- current clients and project stakeholders
- past clients
- staff and potential staff
- new business influencers and referrers
- the architectural sector.

These audiences can be reached through different print, broadcast and online media outlets:

- architectural journals
- construction and technical press
- local newspapers, radio, television and online media (local both to the practice and to the project)
- client/project sector press
- national newspapers, radio, television and online media.

The easiest way to research which press to issue with information is via a media guide. There are a number of online or print guides that list UK and international press covering all outlets – print, broadcast and new media. These guides are regularly updated. An internet search will quickly discover a media guide that offers the best level of information for the practice and its budget. However, these guides can be costly. It may be cheaper to spend some time researching a press list in-house. Ask clients about the key sector journals they read and conduct research using internet search engines to build a bespoke list of target media.

Within the architectural community, the key UK journals include:

- *The Architects' Journal*
- *The Architectural Review*
- *Architecture Today*
- *Blueprint*
- *Building*
- *Building Design*
- *The RIBA Journal*

Approval

Deciding to issue information, whether in a press release, on the firm's website, in a brochure or through a paper given at a conference, is a sensitive matter. As architects, the design and creativity for any project will come from within the practice. However, the project is owned by the client and/or developer. There may also be an end-user or building occupant who could have a view on the content of information presented about the project.

If the project is an especially sensitive one, or there is a date before which no announcements can be made, for whatever reason, the client may impose an embargo and request 100 per cent confidentiality on the project or may ask to see and approve all material prior to issue.

Establish an approval process that should be followed with rigour whenever the practice plans to issue a press release or generate media interest in a project. It is a sensible courtesy to liaise with the client or appropriate stakeholders to obtain approval of the plans and on any written press releases in advance of letting any journalist get so much as a sniff of the material. This precaution can avoid upsetting key client relationships. If in doubt, ask. It is not worth jeopardising a valuable client relationship in order to gain a few column inches in a journal or include an image in a brochure.

Issuing a press release

A press release is information written in the third person that can easily be understood and digested by journalists. In past times, press releases were mailed out to journals, but nowadays they are usually delivered via email and simultaneously posted on the practice's website.

Target press lists need to be identified as recipients for news releases. The cheap way to do this is to search the internet for relevant magazines and build a database of selected editors of the journals that are appropriate for the release. Be sure to include not just architectural titles, but also local print and broadcast media as well as sector journals that will be read by clients.

Sector journals can be tracked down through an internet search. For example, the key journal in the health sector is *Health Service Journal* (HSJ). There are also a number of online media directories than can be accessed for a fee. Subscribing to one of these directories can be a great time saver if the practice is very proactive in issuing stories to a wide range of media. Generating cover for a project, a piece of research, an opinion that affects the sector or expertise that will benefit sector clients, in the industry's own journals, is an effective way of building the practice's brand within that market sector.

Formatting a press release

Journalists may be on the receiving end of hundreds of cold-call emails every week. Make life easier for them by putting the title of the press release into the email message box. Make it snappy and be sure to give the news content of the release. If the message line is vague, be prepared for the release to be deleted without it being opened or read.

On opening the release, the journalist needs to quickly assimilate the news that is being issued. If the release is about a building, a low-resolution image embedded at the top of the email along with an attention grabbing headline will quickly tell the journalist if this is a story worth reading.

Keep the opening paragraph as short and to the point as possible. Try to encapsulate the entire story in one or two sentences. As a rule of thumb, try to keep sentences short in any press release – 25 to 30 words maximum – and no more than three sentences in a paragraph. This is because columns of newsprint are narrow, and 30 words make a four- or five-line paragraph in a magazine such as *The Architects' Journal* or *Building Design*.

Throughout the rest of the release keep all information sharp and to the point. Do not overwrite and do not be tempted to include too much detail or superfluous material. End by giving contact details and information on all platforms in which images are available. If there is extra information that it might be useful for the media to be informed of, but which is not actual news, then include it after the release itself ends, as a 'note to editors'.

A PDF sheet can also be added showing images that can be supplied on request. Do not forget to include the name of the photographer and a copyright confirmation. Be sure that the practice has the right to issue the images to the press. Journals do not take kindly to receiving a bill from a photographer, when the assumption was that clearance to publish an image had been granted, and might well seek payment from the practice.

An example layout for an emailed press release is given in the box below.

For immediate release   Date

Headline

Embedded low-resolution image

* Body text paragraph 1
* Body text paragraph 2
* Body text paragraph 3

Ends

Word count

Contact details

Notes to editors

Attach image sheet as PDF

An example of a complete press release is presented as Appendix 1 to this guide.

Follow up

Issuing a press release is the start of a journey towards getting an item of news published. Calling the titles in which the practice would ideally like the news to appear may increase the chances of the story being published. Having a chat with the editors is always a good idea – it can allow ideas to be put forward for other features which the journal is developing. Don't be afraid to invite the journalist over to the practice to see what is going on and get to know the key people and projects. Editors are as hungry for news as practices are to have their work published.

Forward features

Many journals publish a forward planning features list. This is a plan of issues which the title will look at over the year, primarily issued to help advertisers plan their spending. However, compiling a calendar of the subjects to be covered by target journals over the course of a year can create a useful resource to help plan when to get in touch with editors about a subject on which the practice has useful information, a relevant project to be considered for inclusion or just something to say.

Remember that weekly and monthly journals are planned, written, designed and printed in advance of their cover date. Editorial deadlines can usually be found on the website of each journal, but do not leave it until the last minute to submit information. Working weeks ahead with weekly titles and up to three or four months ahead with a monthly title may increase the chances of a project being considered for publication.

Collecting press cuttings

Checking the journals in the two to three weeks following the issue of a press release is the obvious way to see if the information issued has been used by the media. Searching online editions is also a good way to check on the pickup of a release, but it can be time consuming. However, it is highly unlikely that the practice will subscribe to all the journals to which a press release has been sent. Some practices subscribe to a press cuttings service. Selecting this option can be worthwhile if a lot of press cover is anticipated. Cuttings agencies all have procedures for reading for news items across wide rafts of sector media. Press cuttings will be delivered electronically, and are often supplied with measurable statistics that can be very helpful.

It is a good idea to collect press cuttings in a folder that can be left in the reception or practice waiting space for visitors to browse.

Crisis management

Architecture, like any other service industry, can at times generate bad news. For a practice, this can be anything from a building collapse to a tragedy involving a principal partner, financial difficulties or a demanding lawsuit. It is a good idea to have at least an outline plan mapping out how to proceed if a situation arises that could be picked up by the media. Leaving aside possible legal issues, a crisis can have an immediate impact on the firm's reputation; it could adversely influence the local community, staff and clients and even affect new business wins.

Accidents cannot be anticipated. Other problems, however, can take a while to emerge, meaning that sometimes it is possible to recognise that a crisis is brewing. Contain and manage a crisis by establishing a crisis management plan.

A crisis management plan should identify a management team which is able to make decisions. Things to consider include the following:

- Once the problem has arisen, quickly take the right actions to resolve the situation as far as possible.
- Be seen to act and be seen to care – however, avoid admitting responsibility.
- Keep everyone who needs to be informed fully briefed on the situation.
- Ensure openness and transparency as much as possible, but never admit liability. If in doubt, talk to a lawyer first.
- Prepare a press statement that provides an initial response to the situation. Keep the statement up to date as new details emerge. Show the statement to a lawyer if the situation merits this precaution, but try to avoid issuing information that seems evasive or defensive.
- Check your insurance and/or the contract and, if needs be, take legal advice.
- Keep staff informed.
- Inform clients and key stakeholders about the situation – don't rely on the media to spread the news.

Adverse media coverage

Journals do not always get it right. Every now and again it does happen that a piece can be published where the facts are not accurate, the wrong name may be assigned to a project or the wrong firm given a credit. A typical knee-jerk reaction to a print error about the firm or a project is to call the editor and demand that an erratum notice is published in the next issue to put the record straight. However, this may not always be a good course of action. If the issue is significant, could have an impact on the practice's relationship with a client or seriously damage its reputation, then go ahead. If, however, the misprint is irritating but not significantly damaging, consider letting it ride. Errata acknowledgements for small issues can make the practice seeking redress look mean-spirited. Do, by all means, call the editor and point out the error, but do not seek printed redress. Instead, consider suggesting a meeting to talk over the practice's work, and perhaps angle for a positive piece in the near future looking at another of the firm's projects.

Talking to the press

Giving an interview to a print or broadcast journalist can be a stressful exercise unless some groundwork is done ahead of the meeting. Useful things to remember include:

- be prepared – decide what the three most important things to communicate are, and stick to them
- be prepared for any difficult or obvious questions
- avoid technical jargon and acronyms
- always tell the truth, do not fudge. If an answer cannot be given, or the facts are not known, then say so
- do not be tempted to go 'off the record'
- think answers through and collect your thoughts before answering every question
- do not be tempted to boast or be indiscreet
- keep to the point
- avoid commenting on any industry controversy
- never criticise the work of another company
- use examples that will be relevant to the journal's readership
- do not assume that the journalist will have prior knowledge of or be an expert on the subject
- ask for clarification if the point of a question is not clear
- do not pretend to know all the answers, but offer to find out and send on information that is needed but not available during the interview
- remain factual, do not speculate or offer a hypothesis
- never ask to see the copy before it is published. Journalists will rarely allow sight of copy, unless perhaps the subject matter is very complex, in which case it might be offered for technical accuracy checking only.

If it looks as if the practice is going to be generating plenty of media interest, it is worth organising media training for the people who will be most exposed to the press. Practising how to give an interview to a print or broadcast journalist is always helpful. Not everyone is a natural verbal communicator, and media training will help identify people who will be best able to speak to the press on behalf of the practice.

PR consultants

There comes a time in the life of many business practices when the principals identify the need to raise the bar in terms of the visibility of the firm, and will call on the services of a PR consultant.

PR is a professional communications discipline, with a massive industry supported and regulated by professional organisations, including the Chartered Institute of Public Relations (CIPR) (www.cipr.co.uk), Guild of Public Relations Practitioners (www.prguild.com) and Public Relations Consultants Association (www.prca.org.uk).

Find a PR consultant that has expertise in working with architects and within the built environment sector. A good way to do this is to seek the advice of editors of sector journals. Journalists will always have a view on which PR consultancies give a good service, are switched on to the needs of their clients and issue accurate and well-written information. The CIPR website gives further advice on how to find and appoint a PR consultant. Forms of appointment will vary, ranging from a formal contract and a monthly retainer through to an ad hoc arrangement based on project-by-project initiatives.

Appointing a PR consultant is a big step. To get the most from the appointment, be prepared for the practice principals to be drawn into the process. Understand that time will still have to be set aside in order to brief the consultant about the desired outcomes for a PR initiative. The practice will be expected to supply detailed information and images, and approve draft press statements as the process moves forwards. The PR consultant will expect regular management meetings to keep information flowing and provide updates on ongoing work. Remember, the PR consultant does not work in the practice, and will not know what is going on without being told. If the architects do not pass on the information, the PR consultant cannot get stuck in and deliver against promises that the PR firm made on appointment. The further in advance the consultant can be briefed about an initiative, the better the chances of the information being successfully published.

In conclusion, it is worth remembering that journalists working for industry journals – in the construction sector or in market sectors – are as keen to be the first to generate news items as the practice principals will be to have their work published. Building a relationship with at least one journalist writing for the magazines where the practice needs to see its work published will pay off eventually. However, there is a lot of pressure on printed and web-based journal space these days. Delay making press contact until the practice really has something special to offer to the press. Always make sure that clients are happy for the project to be published. Be realistic and manage expectations. No matter how good the design or the PR consultant, projects that are not top-notch or lack a unique aspect will be hard to place in the media. Remember that not every attempt to generate media coverage for the practice will be successful.

┌──────────────────── **SUMMARY** ────────────────────┐

- Plan PR activities so that they support the business development strategy of the practice.
- Agree key messages that will be used to ensure consistency when presenting the practice to the wider audience.
- Be organised – channel media relations though one point of contact, or consider hiring a PR consultant.
- Understanding the requirements of journal editors will enhance your chances of having your press release published.
- Target a wide range of media, including local press and client sector journals as well as the architectural press.
- Be prepared to deal with any adverse publicity that might arise and develop interview skills to allow you to be confident in dealing with journalists.

└──┘

Section 7
Advertising

John Foster and Charmaine Kimpton, *Shere Marketing*

Advertising is really where marketing began. It used to be the first choice for most businesses trying to raise awareness of their products and services, but it has now become expensive, relative to most other forms of promotion. Nevertheless, it can still be a powerful means of promoting your brand.

Is advertising for you?

The client's decision to purchase advertising is usually a reluctant one. Almost always a compelling need drives the process. Unlike consumer goods purchases, influenced by aspiration and impulse, business purchasing is more rational and considered. Fact gathering, evaluation and often lengthy and exhaustive stages of negotiation are involved in business purchases. Conversely, because time is usually at a premium, a full comprehensive review of options and detailed analysis is frequently bypassed. For these reasons, being well-known in a target market puts an architectural practice at a distinct advantage.

Research shows that business people build a 'mental map' of the marketplace, the service providers they might use and the brands that stand out from the crowd. This is all based on receiving information from a wide variety of sources. Advertising can play a very important part in moving a practice clearly onto this map. The more firmly the practice is established there, the more likely a decision to purchase will be weighted in the firm's favour.

Brand promotion

The focus of advertising should be to reinforce the presence of your brand in the marketplace, underlining its proposition and communicating its identity.

This is often best achieved through showing project work. Demonstrating a proven track record is essential in winning confidence and opening doors.

Advertising architecture or an architectural practice works best when:

- the advertising is part of a practice's long-term brand-building exercise with specific and carefully considered objectives (e.g. to underpin an aggressive business growth strategy or leading up to market listing)
- there is a need to deliver a key message about the practice to a wide audience that cannot be targeted through other marketing means
- it is important to establish the practice brand profile quickly in a given market-place (e.g. to counteract a promotional strategy on the part of a competitor or to take advantage of legislative change that offers a business development opportunity)
- for a major practice announcement (e.g. company name change or acquisition)
- to reposition the practice, highlight specific capabilities or correct a mis-conception
- to support sales activities in reaching new specifiers or market sectors where the practice is not well-established.

Words to the wise

If one is not 100 per cent clear about the target audience that the practice wants to reach through advertising and what the firm is trying to achieve, it is very easy to get the media, the timing and the message wrong.

Always plan to have some proactive public and press relations activities running alongside any advertising. Get the public relations process moving, and then run the advertising as a call-to-action.

Consider how competitors advertise – if competitor firms already have a more convincing story to tell, or have a lot more money to invest, advertising probably should not feature in the smaller practice's marketing toolkit.

It is always important to encourage response, even if the main objective is to deliver a branding message. Key to any advertisement are:#

- an incentive to respond (free portfolio or brochure, receive a paper on design theory, etc.)
- specific telephone and email options or link to website landing page
- main website address.

Different types of advertising

Advertising is principally a means of delivering a message to an audience (Figure 7.1) and can be split into the following categories:

- display: all kinds of paid-for space in publications, plus online banner and panel advertising
- advertorial: sponsored features and supplements
- recruitment: box-type or pay-per-line adverts
- directory listings.

Display, advertorial, sponsored features and supplements

There are many ways to utilise the advertising space that has been purchased, but the objective is always the same – to grab the attention of the reader.

Online advertising through the media, industry portal websites and pay-per-click are advertising tools that every practice should include in its promotional action plan. Unlike offline advertising, these are all directly measurable in terms of return on investment. The same principles of how to develop an effective campaign apply to online as they do to traditional media advertising.

FIGURE 7.1: *Audience delivery mechanisms in advertising*

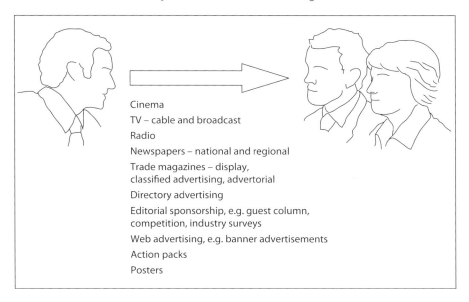

Cinema
TV – cable and broadcast
Radio
Newspapers – national and regional
Trade magazines – display,
classified advertising, advertorial
Directory advertising
Editorial sponsorship, e.g. guest column,
competition, industry surveys
Web advertising, e.g. banner advertisements
Action packs
Posters

Display advertising gives the architectural practice space to present a message exactly as the firm wishes. Sometimes, creating an advert that looks like an editorial ('advertorial') is an option. There are restrictions on how a firm can present an advertorial visually within a journal; for example, publications often insist that the typeface is not the same as the one used for their main editorial content in order to differentiate visually between the journal's editorial and the paid-for advertorial. An advertorial will probably be required to use the heading 'Advertising Feature'.

There are also 'support advertising' and sponsored features. These are opportunities offered by publishers of some magazines to provide support for a profile feature on a particular project or client. Usually this will be offered in publications where independent editorial articles form only a small part of the content.

Advertising such as this, which is usually provided as part of a package with editorial content, can be effective, but never let the publication put the advertisement opposite a feature that the practice has written, as this will clearly flag the fact that the firm has paid for the editorial, thus reducing its authority. Some firms have a set principle of never taking part in this kind of advertising opportunity, believing that it can damage, rather than enhance, their reputation.

Bound-in supplements appearing in high-profile industry publications can give an architectural practice a chance to profile key projects and capabilities and bestow credibility by association. Although more costly than conventional advertisements, supplements offer significant longevity. An added benefit will be the chance to obtain extra copies of the supplement for use as marketing collateral as part of the deal. A key benefit is that the practice will have greater control over what it wants to communicate.

Supplements are particularly useful as a way of raising a firm's profile following major company changes or in the run-up to industry events in which the practice is participating.

Recruitment advertising

Traditional print media is still widely used for recruitment and will continue to challenge online job websites, so the choice of where to advertise a vacancy in the practice is a difficult one.

Attempting to match the competition may be an equally flawed approach. Adopting a 'me too' policy will not help to set the firm apart from others in a crowded marketplace.

Any information or qualitative feedback that the practice receives relating to advertising should be recorded and used as part of the evaluation process when establishing the degree of success of the advertising activity.

Typical return on investment (ROI) metrics that can, additionally, be used to assess value are:

- advertising cost per enquiry/response – not necessarily appropriate for brand advertising where generating sales leads is not the main objective
- reach/coverage – enables detailed analysis of which markets are being exposed to marketing activity.

Benchmark research, in the form of pre- and post-campaign surveys to measure movement in perception and awareness, may ultimately prove the only way to truly evaluate the effectiveness of advertising. However, this can be an expensive exercise and is really only possible for large advertising campaigns. A more achievable route to measuring impact for an architectural practice is to include a question about the visibility and impact of the firm's advertising in its client satisfaction survey.

Choosing media

It is always advisable to limit the number of places in which the practice will advertise. It is better to gain maximum awareness in a few places than minimum awareness in many.

Researching the media prior to planning an advertising schedule is vital. The only way to establish which media are really used by target audiences is to conduct some research, best achieved by talking to contacts, searching the internet for possible magazines and ordering in copies of the key journals being considered for the campaign.

To do this, the practice needs to be certain of the audiences that the advertising is targeting.

Figure 7.3 reflects the diverse range of organisations and job titles that may have an influence in forming attitudes and placing work with a supplier.

FIGURE 7.3: *Target audience*

INFLUENCERS	SPECIFIERS	END-USERS
Construction companies	Developers	Building tenants
Project consultants	Local authorities	Building services and premises managers
Structural engineers	Property investment companies	Facilities managers
Building services engineers	Major client companies	Facilities management companies
Energy management consultants		Local community
Property management companies		Local authorities
Local planning authorities		Commercial business community
		Built environment community

Once the audience to be reached is established, and the media that might be used have been identified, a thorough examination of both data sets is essential.

Sources of information include:

• media packs – carefully review the publication's interests and values, key focus areas and coverage by job title and type of organisation
• circulation figures – the more credible publishing houses open up their circulations to vigorous auditing. Circulation certification provides a valuable stamp of authority, confirming that the magazine is indeed circulated to the audience it claims to reach, although this audit is merely proof of postage. A publication's actual readership feedback is always more important than its circulation figures.

Auditing organisations include the following:

• ABC (www.abc.org.uk), owned by the media industry, independently verifies and reports on media performance across print, events, digital and evolving platforms
• BPA Worldwide (www.bpaww.com) is a global industry resource for verified audience data and media knowledge.

Commercial versus controlled circulation?

Editorial quality in controlled circulation magazines may be as high if not higher than 'paid-for' titles, but be sure to choose publications operating a 'requested' policy.

- Readership survey research conducted by individual publications can be biased, both in the use of leading questions and in data presentation.
- The strength of a publication in terms of influence with its audience must be determined. The circulation figure is not a reliable indicator. Incisive and authoritative editorial suggests a serious and senior readership. Glossy and beautiful may not always gain the attention of decision-makers.
- Avoid titles which are read solely by architects and the design profession – do not make the mistake of using media that is speaking only to the firm's peer group.
- Many leading titles based in the UK have an international distribution or are increasing their international focus. Careful selection will achieve comprehensive UK and global coverage.
- Be wary of advertising representatives who try to persuade architects to take out advertising 'because so-and-so is there', but do factor such information into the research and adjust planning based on the positive (or negative) impact that advertising has on target audiences for key competitors.

The schedule

How often should the advertisement appear? There are no hard and fast rules about the frequency of running advertisements although, obviously, budget will dictate this to some extent.

A rule of thumb is that an advertisement needs to appear in three consecutive issues for the average reader to have seen it once.

What kind of advertising?

The following box lists all the common permutations of types of advertising available within trade publications.

Advertising options

In book:
Half page
Single page
Double page
Centre four pages with run-on options

Special positions/types:
Front cover sponsorship
Back page
Inside front/back cover

Inserts:
Loose insert
Bound insert
Outsert (cover wraparound)

Other:
Sole-sponsored issue
Bellyband/wraparound
Subscription promotions
Polybag sponsorship

Joint initiatives:
Competitions
Editorial sponsorships, e.g. columns, industry surveys

Research by the publisher Reed on the way that people read magazines and what effect placement has in capturing initial attention and duration of study made the following observations.

- The average person spends just seconds scanning advertisements – double-page spreads do not necessarily generate twice the attention span, making single-page, or even half-page ads, more cost effective.
- Inside covers and pages 2 and 3 are often sold at a premium but are subject to the risk of 'flickability'.

- Back pages can offer high initial visibility – when taken out of a wrapper magazines often lie back to front, giving the advertisement an immediate opportunity to shout at a buyer, and will be seen repeatedly where magazines are kept for reference purposes. There is also the coffee-table factor, when magazines can be left lying face down.
- Front page sponsorship is likely to prove more valuable in the context of public relations, usually giving cover line links to the page on which the editorial appears.
- Advertising appearing in the early news pages or opposite/within relevant features may well increase the likelihood of being seen, as readers will spend more time studying these pages.
- Right-hand pages tend to be scanned first by readers, therefore ads on a right-hand page may outperform those on left-hand pages (although booking early left-hand pages is better than booking right-hand pages towards the back of the magazine).
- Half-page advertisements – there is some evidence also to suggest that advertisements on the outer/top edges of the page offer an advantage, although a much more important issue is to secure a 'solus' position on the page alongside editorial matter rather than other advertisements. This guarantee is what gives single-page advertisements the edge over half pages.
- Don't be afraid to be creative. A run of strips or half pages in a single issue may deliver more impact for not much more than single-page rates (however, some publishers operate policies which may restrict your options).

Media buying

Here are some points to bear in mind when booking advertising:

- Be very specific about where the advertisement is to appear. Without a clear direction about location in the magazine, the advertisement will be positioned as 'run of paper', which means it could be placed anywhere.
- Do not pay extra for specified positions other than covers and 'specials'.
- Late booking can pay off, as publishers will offer lower rates closer to closing deadlines – however, this is a high-risk tactic as the advertisement may not get the best choice of space.
- Develop advertising artwork to a number of different sizes and formats and have them on hand to allow the practice to take advantage of special

offers (but resist the temptation to take deals that do not fit in with the firm's advertising strategy).
- Make sure that the price is negotiable with the publication – rarely does anyone 'buy off the rate card' (i.e. at the prices which publishers quote).

Creative

Advertisements based on solid facts have been proven to outperform clever copy – a triumph of substance over style. However, poorly executed copy and design, no matter how strong the proposition, will flop because the advertisement itself will not attract attention.

The most important aspect, surprisingly often forgotten, is that unless the advertisement reaches out and grabs the attention of the reader, it is not doing its job and its impact will be low.

Three guiding principles for developing an advertisement are outlined below:

- Attention grab is 70 per cent visual, 30 per cent headline – an eye-catching visual theme is essential.
- Headlines are only compelling when they make a connection with a genuine issue or need.
- Use key benefits in the first lines of the copy to draw the reader in.

When starting the process of developing an advertisement, begin by stepping into the reader's shoes. Imagine flicking through the magazine or online resource in which the advert is to appear. What grabs the attention?

Once it is decided how the advertisement is to look, the audience it is trying to reach, where it will be placed and for how long the campaign will run, the time comes to develop the content.

Start with a really hard look at what the advertisement is trying to achieve.

Is there a unique selling proposition (USP)? Are there specific features offered by the practice that differentiate it from the competition? Look carefully at the practice's values and attributes and identify the reasons why clients are draw to the firm.

Is the practice better in terms of:

- value
- quality

- customer relationships
- problem-solving/advice/tenacity
- innovation
- reliability
- proven track record/longevity
- sustainable approach
- project delivery
- sector experience
- award winning design
- high-profile projects
- investment in IT
- regional presence
- sector experience.

Some publications will offer to design the artwork for advertisements from copy and images supplied. While this can seem to offer a saving, relinquishing control of the design development of an advert may lead to a failure to apply the practice's brand. Most architectural firms have someone with graphic design skills in-house. If not, consider using a graphic design agency.

Advertising agencies

The key question to ask is: does the practice have the skills in-house to create good, original advertising concepts and copy, and to manage an advertising campaign?

Developing and executing a successful advertising campaign will require:

- media research and planning, and space buying (advertising agencies usually have greater purchasing power and expertise in negotiating discounts)
- copywriting, design and art direction
- management to ensure delivery of artwork to schedule, in the required format, to diverse publications and online media.

If specialist assistance is required on some aspects of the process, then there are plenty of highly capable advertising agencies out there. Beware though – if the practice principals firmly believe that the practice can develop and manage its own advertising, it means that any relationship with an agency could well be difficult.

Finding the right advertising agency

If the practice is already working with a public relations or marketing agency, check to see if the service supplier offers advertising expertise. Buying an advertising service from an existing supplier can improve integration between the practice's various marketing activities and speed up delivery (as there will be no learning curve for the consultancy to follow), and using just one supplier will probably also achieve savings.

If the practice decides to look for a new advertising agency, begin by compiling a list of up to ten potential firms, then do a website review to establish if there is a good 'fit' with your practice. Make calls to a few industry contacts and journalists to seek referrals to advertising agencies that are active in the built environment sector and so are more likely to understand how to create an appropriate campaign for an architectural practice.

Narrowing down the list

- Does the advertising agency genuinely specialise in architecture and the built environment? There is no substitute for in-depth understanding of the firm's primary business sector and the building procurement process.
- Location – working with an agency will involve face-to-face meetings, and time is money. Pick a firm that is within range.
- Is the agency the right size? If an agency has a blue-chip client list of very large organisations it may mean that the account of an architectural practice may not get the attention it deserves.
- Ask to meet the people who will manage the account on a day-to-day basis, not just the pitch team.
- Establish what reporting and monitoring systems the agency has in place.

Once a shortlist of agencies is settled (selecting no more than three agencies is advisable), decide if there is the need for a speculative pitch. If the total budget is substantial and the practice intends to run a long-term campaign, it is reasonable to request this.

Issuing the advertising brief

- Write a brief, but keep it short. Advertising agencies respond best to a concise set of key criteria.

- Include a summary of the thinking behind the need for the campaign and bullet points covering background, history and ethos of your practice, business objectives, target audiences, rationale for advertising, budget, plus any other key essential factors. Do not hold back information and do offer to respond to further questions.
- Allow sufficient time. No agency will respond well to a last-minute brief for an important advertising campaign. Neither best ideas nor a solid response will be forthcoming unless adequate time is allowed.

Making the advertising decision and working with the agency

- When reviewing the work, keep the decision-making group small. Committee decisions on creative work usually lead to a safe solution that will not grab the intended audience's attention.
- Never make the decision after long consideration. Any potential client will not analyse an advertisement – they will react to it. Trust first reactions to the advertising concepts presented by the agencies.
- Try to see the practice's advertising from an outside perspective.
- Never ask people who are not immersed in the architecture and the built environment sector to help decide what advertising the practice should use.

Be very clear in all communications with the agency, at all times. The discipline of precision in this area is just as important as it is in communication between the architectural practice and its clients.

The relationship will occasionally be difficult. Allow for the fact that a good agency will challenge the brief and be open to this.

In conclusion, advertising can showcase the architectural work delivered to date, but to consistently drive up the volume of sales leads coming in to the practice, other proactive activity, such as direct marketing, website promotion and public relations, will also be needed.

SUMMARY

- Advertising works best as part of a long-term practice brand-building exercise.
- Plan other proactive activities to run alongside any advertising campaign.
- Advertising requires time to deliver meaningful change to the brand and reputation of the practice within the marketplace.
- Plan any advertising carefully. Occasional and one-off adverts will not have great impact on the target sector.
- Carefully match output media to targeted audiences.
- Be creative in the development of content. Remember that attention grab for an advertisement is 70 per cent visual and 30 per cent headline.

Section 8
Successful award entries

David Crawford, *Technical Editorial Consultancy*

Winning a design award (a full award, commendation or mention) is a highly exploitable success story for an architectural practice. But the thinking about how to include an award win in the marketing of the practice should, ideally, start at the time of the decision to submit a project to an award scheme. This will help to maximise the chances of a successful outcome.

Entering an award scheme is a marketing exercise in its own right. By taking part, the practice is deciding to submit the quality of its work to the test of independent criticism and judgement.

The assessment process may well involve not just fellow design professionals but also lay-representatives of client or user communities. It is therefore important to bear their interests in mind from the outset when preparing an award entry.

Adopting a marketing-aware approach will add convincing focus and clarity to the entry. To the same end, practices need to keep themselves abreast of changes in the thinking behind design awards.

The value of awards

Winning an architectural design award has substantial, long-term marketing value for the practice – influencing client perceptions, enhancing the firm's professional profile and supporting efforts in staff retention and recruitment. An award win will:

- give external recognition to the overall quality and performance of a practice's work

- secure wider (or continued) awareness of the creative skills of the firm within a competitive marketplace
- impart pride and confidence to partners and staff
- establish the practice's competence in designing specific building types or solutions.

Some schemes also give monetary awards; for example, the RIBA Stirling Prize.

Future Systems, which won £20,000 in 1999 for the NatWest Media Centre at Lord's Cricket Ground in London, is on record as recognising the importance of the money, which was won at a critical stage in the company's development.

Reasons to enter an awards scheme

The time, money and effort that a practice has expended on entering an award scheme should not be written off as wasted if the entry is unsuccessful.

Offsetting compensations arising from going through the process of developing an award entry include:

- learning (or becoming better informed) about the awards process, putting the practice in a stronger position to enter future schemes
- benefiting from the judgement of the assessors, by using their reports to evaluate and perhaps reappraise the practice's approach to collateral design and presentation
- developing the discipline of revisiting a brief and describing a project convincingly in tightly written summaries with high-quality illustrations. (Once produced, of course, this material remains available for promotional use, while the experience of preparing and producing it is of continuing value.)

Practices can use these subsidiary outcomes to advantage.

Information on award schemes

There was formerly no generally available, centrally maintained and updated database of award schemes open to architects practising in the UK, however the RIBA now includes a comprehensive list on its Awards website.

A representative checklist of some built-environment sector award schemes appears in Appendix 2, page 161.

Choosing which award scheme(s) to enter

There are currently well over 100 design award schemes operating at varying levels. The main categories are:

- international awards
- national awards (open)
- national awards (restricted; for example, to building type or building material used)
- regional and local awards (for example, schemes run by RIBA regions, local authorities or civic societies).

Practices should equip themselves in advance with all the available information on the schemes they plan to enter. Being well-informed about the published assessors and their methods of judging can be a useful preliminary.

Studying the results of previous scheme entries will also give useful insights on those that offer the best chances of success – or are likely to be most useful to the practice's marketing strategy.

The RIBA website gives information about past winners of its awards, as an element in an Institute-wide database development programme designed, inter alia, to allow genuine online entry.

For a practice with little or no previous experience of the awards process, entering a local scheme can be a valuable exercise. Such schemes often have the advantage of minimal formality. The Camden Design Awards, run every other year by the London borough to promote local awareness of high-quality design, aim to be 'as open as possible' within a six-month qualifying period. Anyone can nominate and there are no building-type categories.

There will often be scope for entering the same project in more than one award scheme. The best way to minimise resulting increases in time and costs is to rationalise the effort and avoid duplication by planning ahead and aggregating entry requirements (especially when it comes to the expense of photography). At the same time, documentary material will require careful editing to meet the particular entry conditions for each award.

Comparing the requirements for a number of schemes can also help to improve the quality of an individual entry. Some, for example, may place specific emphasis on factors such as building performance, community, accessibility or sustainability issues. Taking account of these elements in schemes that are not so specific can help to produce a more rounded and convincing entry.

Restrictions in award schemes

Specific schemes may impose important restrictions on submissions. Examples are:

- membership of professional or other bodies – the RIBA Awards, for example, require an individual entrant to be a chartered member of the RIBA, RIAS, RSUA or RSAW, or an international (honorary) fellow of the RIBA; or the practice entering to have at least one full-time principal who is a chartered member of any of these institutions
- materials used – a scheme run by a trade association may restrict entries to buildings that use products from its member companies
- geographical – a regional or local scheme should specify precise qualifying boundaries
- qualifying periods – these can vary widely; for example, one scheme may state that a project may be entered at any point within a period of, say, three years from its completion time, while another may require a building to be complete and occupied by the time of submission.

Again, schemes may or may not allow the submission of more than one project in a single category or the entry of the same project in more than one category.

Clearance and authentication

Client consent is often a prerequisite for award scheme entry, as is the consent of the client and of the building occupier for taking award-specific photography and making arrangements for assessors' site visits. Other likely requirements are for photographers' written permission for publicity use and for specialist authentication. It is important to ensure that the firm has copyright permission from the photographer for all images submitted in an award entry, and an agreement that the images can be used on a royalty-free basis by the award organiser.

The RIBA Awards, for example, stipulate – as part of a section on building performance in use – a sign-off, by an environmental engineer, of energy use figures and statistics for all projects over a specified contract value. Clearances and consents will also be necessary for media releases and other marketing material following a success, so it is important to retain relevant contact details.

Qualifying dates

The dates will always need careful checking. The RIBA Awards conditions, for example, require that a submitted project must be completed and occupied by the award entry deadline, and state that 'jurors will expect to see evidence of occupation'.

Again, a scheme may specify that a project may be entered only once within a qualifying period of a given number of years from its completion. Architects should, therefore, try to weigh up their chances of success in any given year before deciding when to submit a project.

Documentary requirements

Written project descriptions that accompany an award entry are normally restricted in length. This means that these crucial texts must be to the point. Schemes typically allow between 100 and 500 words. Making the most of a tight word allowance is a real test of effective communication, presentational and marketing skills.

The description should be written in plain English and broken down into relevant sections, each clearly sub-headed to show how the information meets specific scheme criteria. It should also spell out how the entry contributes to the scope of the scheme (for example, in the use of materials, workability for a given business sector or respect for/enhancement of the local environment). Ensure that any guidance on required information about the project given in the entry notes is followed to the letter.

There can be special requirements for information on, for example, the building's performance in use and compliance with inclusive design principles. It will help the assessors' appreciation of the entry if it references accompanying illustrations in the text.

Apart from increasing the chances of success, careful preparation of documentation will provide the basis for future media and other publicity material.

Image requirements

Colour photography should be first class. The 2009 Brick Awards entry form states that: 'Entrants should bear in mind that initial assessments will be made on the evidence of the photographic material submitted with the entry, so excellent images are essential!'. The importance of high-quality photography cannot be overstated.

Photographs should show the building in use, as well as in an architecturally pristine condition, even if not specifically requested.

Drawing sets may need to include directional maps, site or location plans. Images may, additionally, be required on disk.

Ensure that copyright permission for all images submitted with the award entry is obtained in advance and provide any photographic credits that may be needed to accompany the images.

Submitting an entry – checklist

Key points to check are:

- the deadline (allowing a sufficient margin of error for delivery)
- the submission medium (printed/electronic)
- requirements for material to be in more than one format (for example, images submitted on CD as well as individually)
- evidence of necessary clearances and permissions
- scope for making multiple entries.

Publicising awards

Scheme organisers have their own rules on, and arrangements for, publicising results and entrants may be formally required to cooperate with these. The RIBA states that: 'Submission of an entry will be taken to imply the granting of permission to publish all material and particulars of the successful schemes, including the jury report'. It goes on to reserve 'the right to disqualify any entry which is subject to unauthorised disclosure prior to the official announcements'.

The practice can, however, usually publicise the fact that it has entered a scheme, had it shortlisted, etc., throughout the process (many organisers themselves publish shortlists). In its 2009 Awards brochure, the Royal Institution of Chartered Surveyors, which operates its award scheme through regional heats, asked: 'What more effective marketing tool is there than the publicity of entering, let alone the recognition of winning, one of the property industry's most important and prestigious showcases?'

A successful practice can, and should, take full advantage of the time between an early notification in confidence and the public announcement to plan ahead for optimum marketing use of the award. Always ensure that there is an update on the firm's website that is ready to go live to coincide with the announcement.

"plan ahead for optimum marketing use of the award"

Issue a press release announcing the win to:

- architectural and design media
- sectoral media used by the project client
- professional media used by project co-consultants
- trade media used by major contractors and suppliers
- public sector media dealing with environmental, infrastructural, sustainability and accessibility issues
- appropriate national, regional and local press.

Entering for a design award is itself a marketing exercise. It can lead on to further marketing opportunities if the project is successful, but is still capable of providing useful information even if it is unsuccessful. Treating the entire sequence of events as a continuing marketing exercise will deliver worthwhile benefits.

SUMMARY

- Be strategic when selecting which award schemes to enter.
- Check the award scheme's criteria carefully before starting work on the entry.
- Ensure that all approvals and copyright permissions are gained before submitting the entry.
- Check that the project dates match the entry criteria.
- Follow the rules on submission length and presentation accurately.

Section 9
The measurement of success

Helen Elias, *AECOM*

The brand of the firm, how it positions itself in the marketplace and how it chooses to build its reputation, is an intangible asset that is difficult to quantify. Yet, it is also an extremely valuable asset, so it is worth attempting to measure brand success wherever possible. This section explores some ways to assess the success of the marketing efforts.

The perception of the practice in the marketplace

The construction industry thrives on personal relationships. The success of an architectural practice rests on building the reputation of the firm within the wider marketplace. Once work is won, the way in which the work is delivered, degrees of creativity and innovation, even how people behave at meetings can all influence client perception of the practice.

The construction industry generates a large proportion of repeat business. It is a generally received wisdom within the industry that it can cost about five times as much in terms of time, effort and money to win a new piece of business from a new client, compared with retaining an existing client and generating repeat business.

In a competitive marketplace, it is vital for a practice to understand fully what it is that it is doing right – in terms of marketing, client relationship management, creativity and service delivery. Just as significant, however, is an understanding of any areas in which the firm is underperforming – which might lead to clients being receptive to an approach from a competitor when the next project is being considered. Perceptions about individual people can influence clients' perceptions about an entire company.

Hearing the client's point of view about how service levels could be improved is a cornerstone to any practice that is serious about winning work, retaining clients and generating repeat business.

Taking the time to understand what makes a client satisfied is an effort worth making. After all, the success of the practice is based on its reputation. Reputation is not a physical, tangible asset. One bad experience can lead to a wave of rumour and disparaging remarks circulating around the industry. The perception of a poor reputation can have a negative impact on potential new clients and decision-makers.

An average client is quite likely to tell at least ten other key contacts about a bad experience with an architectural practice. Each of these ten potential customers has not only been influenced, but could well pass on negative feedback to a further five potential customers in their own circle of contacts. Suddenly, at least 60 potential clients or influencers have been directly, and negatively, influenced.

The majority of customers who have a bad experience with a practice will not do any further business with it. Yet few unsatisfied clients will bother to tell the failing architectural practice exactly where it went wrong. Without this knowledge, the architects cannot make reparation – and may even make the same mistake with other clients.

The ripple effect caused by talking about a negative experience with a practice can continue to circulate poor impressions around the industry long after the building has opened and the main project team has been disbanded and moved on. Nipping bad impressions in the bud to prevent any opportunity for the development of a poor reputation can only happen when there is a clear understanding of what the practice has done wrong, or, more subtly, was not exactly getting right.

Measuring the impact of marketing

Marketing is frequently described as a 'grey area'. It is hard to measure just how successful all the hard work and time spent promoting the practice across its selected platforms and outlets has really been. It is important to be able to assess, as far as possible, a return on investment (ROI), which marketing initiatives have worked for the firm and which activities have not delivered against expectations in a meaningful way. However, not every investment in marketing will generate an ROI – setting up a client database is vital to marketing efficiency, but can it have a measure of impact attached to it?

Some measurement metrics do exist that can be applied to certain aspects of marketing communication activities.

Client feedback

Understanding customers is a key driver that will sit at the heart of the practice. Ultimately, the most accurate way to quantify the effectiveness of public relations and marketing activities, irrespective of the platform used to communicate a message, is to survey the target audience to check what goes down well and what has not worked. One way to ensure that the firm is always seeking to improve its

"Understanding customers is a key driver"

service levels and build ever-closer relationships with clients is to check regularly to see that the clients are, in fact, fully satisfied with the service they are getting.

Using the quality management system for feedback

Many architectural practices see the feedback process as a box that has to be ticked in order to keep their quality management system (QMS) accreditation. A basic QMS system will be based on a feedback form that asks a set of questions about the development and delivery of a project. Somewhere on that form will be found a question or two about the way that the practice has communicated with the client, including marketing initiatives. The answers are usually requested on a score basis – where the lowest number indicates poor satisfaction and the highest number indicates excellent service.

It is common practice for the form to be sent to the client at project close out, along with a hopeful letter from the practice asking for it to be completed and returned. A few replies will come back as a result, but the return level of a mailed out satisfaction form is usually low. The statistical data from the completed forms that are returned will be logged on a spreadsheet, with the forms archived in case of audit.

Clause 8.2.1 of ISO 9001 is quite clear about the measurements of customer satisfaction that should be achieved under QMS: 'the organisation shall monitor information relating to customer perception as to whether the organisation has met customer requirements.' Although there is no specific requirement to perform formal customer satisfaction surveys to meet ISO 9001, the auditor will look to see that the practice has a transparent customer feed-back process in place, which includes relevant, representative and reliable information that can be analysed effectively, with the results used to drive continual improvement.

Client satisfaction surveys

Increasing numbers of architectural practices are now taking the customer satis-faction process seriously. The outcomes from an in-depth survey are illuminating, even if the information uncovered is not what the architects running the practice may want to hear. An interview with a firm with which the practice believes it has an excellent relationship can produce unexpected comments on service level, performance, attitude of staff or other issues that might be unsettling and need addressing. Negative feedback prompts action, and should be viewed as an opportunity to introduce improvements. Practices that have an established client satisfaction process in place are able to more directly hone staff personal development, project management, submission and bids documents, marketing strategies and even management of meetings, presentations and difficult situations as a result.

The opportunity to really see things from a customer's side of the table should not be ignored. A business relationship should not be taken for granted, as complacency can lead to a lowering in standards of service. Likewise, as the practice grows, opens offices, employs more staff and increases service offers, satisfaction surveys are a good tool for checking that key clients are aware of the practice's enhanced capability. Never assume that clients know what changes the practice is making. Find out what they know, and what they don't know.

The first step is to agree what the firm wants to achieve from a fully fledged customer satisfaction process. Establishing desired outcomes will ensure that feedback collected is going to be of use. Develop the right questions to ask to deliver feedback that can be used to influence long-term management of the practice and enhance client relationships, covering all key professional relationships as well as client organisations. Agree a process at the start for sharing feedback, so that those responsible for developing marketing, staff training, business development and running projects all get to hear the things that are most relevant.

Satisfaction can be measured in many ways:

- service level
- value for money
- creativity
- skill in discipline
- meetings management and behaviour
- personality
- professionalism
- fee levels
- office environment
- attitude
- accessibility
- marketing and communication.

Methods for collecting client feedback

There are many different ways to collect the feedback, so it is important to decide which system, or combination of systems, is best for the practice. The most frequently used formats are:

- face-to-face interviews
- telephone interviews
- questionnaires sent by post or email.

At this point, decide whether the practice wants to gather the information itself or use an independent consultant to make the calls or visit the client for a face-to-face interview. The process that is deployed will, to a certain extent, dictate the format for the questions themselves.

Questionnaires by post or email are best structured as scored questions on which the client can easily make judgements. The results can be analysed statistically, but give little scope for interpretation or personal views. At least 20 to 30 completed forms will be needed in order to get a representative sample to reveal trends in answers that make the exercise worthwhile. Posted or emailed questionnaires frequently get lost or are simply ignored, so expect a lower return from this route.

Another option is to gather information by phone. This process best suits a score-style questionnaire, although it does allow room for personal observations as well. Many people dislike being kept on the phone for a long time, so restrict the questionnaire to take less than 15 minutes.

The most in-depth analysis of the practice from a client's point of view will come from qualitative one-to-one interviews. Approach clients and ask for an hour, then send in the practice's representative armed with a raft of five or six conversational leads to trigger information flow about the areas that really matter – service levels, professionalism, creativity, personal relationships

"trigger information flow about the areas that really matter"

and staff performance are usually included. The conversation may also provide feedback on other areas such as IT capability, finance systems, marketing and press impact.

It only takes five or six in-depth interviews using this route for themes to begin to emerge, touching on areas that the practice might have suspected would arise, or uncovering new areas that can come as a bit of a surprise. Clustering results from the interviews can give recognition to the practice's strengths, while identifying areas where there is room for improvement. Clients seem to like being asked to give feedback in this way, and even the busiest of people will set aside time, as they can see the benefits to their future working relationships with the practice.

Do not be complacent about the firms that are surveyed – it is tempting to send the interviewer to speak to people that the architectural principals know will send back a positive message. But is there anything to be learned from this? More constructive information can be gained by being brave enough to explore the service offer of the practice with past clients, and clients with ongoing projects where things may have run into problems. Pick clients strategically from different market sectors and geographical locations, or served by different offices or design disciplines.

Delivery process for this form of measurement must be both professional and efficient. Make sure that the whole system is set up professionally; start by sending personal letters asking for the interview. Send a letter of thanks immediately after the interview, and another a few months later send a follow-up letter explaining how the feedback gained has been collected and used to help the development of the practice.

It is to the responsibility of any firm that wants to keep repeat business coming in to make sure that service levels and all other aspects of client-facing activities are monitored, and that clients are constantly consulted to make sure that everything is satisfactory. Do not wait until something has gone wrong to send in the client satisfaction interviewer. Make sure that a client is happy with the way that the project is moving along. In the competitive construction sector, where there are plenty of other architects to choose from, forewarned is forearmed. Identify problems and iron them out before they become major issues that can influence a client and create an obstruction to any future work.

SUMMARY

- Understand the importance of ensuring that the work and service delivery provided by the practice is meeting client expectations.
- Take the time to understand what is needed to keep a client satisfied for current projects, to sow the seeds for repeat business.
- Record what clients think – what works, what does not work about the practice offer and delivery levels – and use the feedback to inform the development of the practice.
- Use the quality management system and other feedback procurement routes to generate useful data that can be acted upon.
- Inform clients and staff of any changes to the business that evolve from taking the feedback on board.

Section 10
Publishing a book about the practice

Alex Harvie, *publishing and writing consultant*

Whatever the motivation, embarking on the creation of a book is a major undertaking for any architectural practice. This section provides a guide to the process. Beginning with the initial thinking a practice needs to do before creating a book, the section goes on to outline the two primary publishing methods and, finally, to explain technical issues, from the need to check contract arrangements to types of binding.

The idea of publishing a book can arise when:

- an architectural practice feels the need for a coherent, well-presented document to demonstrate its experience and capabilities to clients
- a milestone anniversary is approaching
- a significant project has been undertaken that deserves particular explanation
- the practice wants to explore and communicate particular theories
- the practice has undergone a rebrand or change of focus.

Getting started

Below is a series of questions which should help the practice to develop the initial brief for a book. The questions are not exhaustive and it may not be possible to answer every one at the outset, but flagging up issues early on should reduce problems later.

Who is the audience?

It is essential to decide who the practice is trying to communicate with: it could be partners and architects within the practice, it could be future clients or it could be the wider architectural community. Define the audience as clearly as possible. Trying to reach multiple audiences leads to confused, unsatisfactory communication because each group's information needs are specific. With an audience in mind, the book's tone of voice becomes obvious. Using a book as a brochure is a popular marketing technique within the architectural profession. A book gives the opportunity for a practice to present its design approach, culture and creativity in a way that a brochure alone cannot.

What is the book for?

What does the publication hope to achieve? How will it be used? How long will it be needed? When will the information be updated? There is no bigger waste than spending a large sum of money on a book which is out of date before it has recouped its costs. There is no guarantee that a book will sell in sufficient quantities to generate a profit, so planning a financial return is not a sufficient reason to embark on a publication. That the book might make a loss is more likely to be the case. Given the time and money involved in the production of a book, it is important to be clear about the benefits to reputation that the practice may reap from such a significant investment. How a practice calculates the benefits will vary between practices. It might be in terms of hard deals won on the back of the book, or a perceived shift in how the practice's philosophy is articulated in the broader market. It is usually the case that practices find that a book helps them to gain an enormous amount in terms of raised profile with peers and clients, providing a prestigious marketing tool to hand out in the process. Whatever the particular perceived benefit may be, it is important for the practice to have discussed the project's parameters for success at the outset.

What is the content?

What does the book have to say? Is it an overview of projects? Is there anything new in the material? Is there an interesting way of structuring the content – for example, by breaking down the work according to theme, or a linking concept? It is important to develop a clear and interesting premise to grab the reader's attention and encourage them to follow the argument from first principle to latest innovation.

"What does the book have to say?"

While the best books are always in some way unique, practices should avoid trying to be too clever. Even the most erudite reader will find it hard to follow work which is not logically organised. A good book manages to transfer information regardless of the fact that many visual people tend to read in a non-linear way (some might flick through images, others might start at the back). Finding an interesting way of structuring the content is crucial to a book's success.

What is the budget?

The practice needs to be very clear about how much money it is prepared to spend. The cost of different approaches to publishing varies significantly.

When is the book needed?

Commercial publishing has a long lead time. Some publishers quote at least nine months to produce a book, others between 12 and 18 months. This time-scale allows for the concept to be refined and developed and for design work to be undertaken.

If the practice requires a book more quickly than this, a publisher may still be willing to take the project on. However, the project will disrupt the publisher's cycle of work and, inevitably, cost more money to produce, so it will come down to the book's particular merits and the deal which is struck. A practice with a limited time-scale might find it best to consider self-publishing as a means of gaining control over time-scales. Printing itself is a relatively quick process; generally it is all the other work which takes the time. If a practice is prepared to give the creation of the book priority within its own schedules it will be able to ensure that deadlines are met.

Research

Research the market by browsing the shelves of specialist book shops and searching on the internet. When interesting books have been gathered they should be analysed systematically in order to refine the initial brief.

This information should help to build up a clear picture of the kind of book the practice would like to create.

Analysing existing publications

Design
- Which book is the best designed?
- What is it about the layout that works?
- Does it come close to the feel and style the practice would like to achieve?
- How much text is there or is it mainly images?

Photography
- Which book has the best photographs?
- What feelings do the images convey?
- Who took them?

Content
- Are the books straightforward catalogues of work or do they have something else behind the way they are structured?
- Do any of the books have particularly accessible thinking?
- Do any of them have an interesting combination of drawings and diagrams to explain processes?
- Are any of them particularly easy to navigate? How do they achieve this – chapter headings, topics, colours on the pages?

Packaging
- Look at the feel of the paper, the text and colours.
- Look at the formats of the books. What size are they? What do you like/dislike about the different sizes?
- Try reading the books with and without a desk to place them on.
- Look at the covers. Are they hard or soft?
- Look at the binding. Do the pages open easily so photographs and images can be seen right to the join?

Contacts
- Note the publishers of the books selected.
- Are any design companies listed? If no designer is named, was the design undertaken in-house by the publisher? Or was it the architect's work?
- Who wrote the book?

Getting published

While architectural books vary widely in content, tone and design – from philosophic treatises to catalogues of new work and explorations of new technologies and practices – there are two principal routes by which they come into existence:

- *commercial publishing* – a proposal is accepted as financially viable in the market-place by a publisher, who then funds and manages the book's publication
- *self-publishing* – a practice decides to fund and create a book in-house and takes on the necessary work itself.

Some recent developments in the market mean there is more overlap in these routes than before, but at a fundamental level they still split the basic modes of production.

Self-sponsored publication is an option whereby a publisher provides a 'publishing service' for the practice, producing the book to high standards but then passing the stock back to the practice at a pre-agreed price. This option is ideal in cases where the market may not be strong enough to justify a book being offered for sale, but still allows the practice to benefit from a high-quality book for its own dissemination. The publisher may assist by helping to place the book in bookshops as well, but without the expectation that bookshop sales alone will underwrite the cost of the book's production.

Commercial publishing

Commercially published architectural books usually come about when a practice approaches a publisher with an idea which the publisher deems to be financially viable. These books go on sale to the public.

Architectural publishing is a unique market and it is important to acknowledge its particular characteristics.

Architectural books are expensive to produce

They need to hold their own in an extremely design-conscious market. Their cost comes from their high production values (the quality of printing and paper stock) as well as the work that goes into designing and writing them.

Sales are limited

Hardly any architectural books make it to the high street. Most bookshops interpret architecture through history (stocking historical overviews and books on a few extremely well-known architects) or through lifestyle (books on interior design are placed on the architecture shelf). Books about current architects, their thinking and their work very rarely make it to mass-market outlets.

In spite of this, there is a thriving trade

A significant number of interesting and innovative architectural books are published every year. It is a fundamental means by which architects communicate their ideas in a fast-moving global arena. This thriving architectural book trade can be found in:

- specialist book shops (such as RIBA Bookshops, the Architectural Association bookshop, Foyles, some museum bookshops)
- booksellers over the internet (such as www.ribabookshops.com)
- specialist private libraries in some larger organisations
- university libraries
- some public libraries.

The book will remain in the public arena

An important consideration for a practice thinking of approaching a publisher is to decide whether it is the right time to place a book in the commercial realm. Some publishers feel that practices rush the publication of their first book and that this makes it difficult further down the line when the practice is ready to have more significant books published on their work. Once a book is in the marketplace it can't be retracted. A practice in its early stages might be better to first try the self-publishing or self-sponsoring route described in the next section, limiting their distribution until they are entirely ready to make a lasting statement.

Commercial publishers find other ways of offsetting costs

Volumes of sales for this specialist field are modest in comparison with the wider publishing trade, which means that, from a publisher's perspective, the financial risk of producing the book is higher. In other areas of publishing, the publisher would reduce production values, thereby limiting the outlay on design and materials and so minimising the risk. However, as an industry, architecture demands high quality, and its publishing houses have had to find ways round this problem.

- Some publishers limit their range to books on well-known practices and common topics and theories; in effect, guaranteeing a return on their investment.
- Some publishers ask for a contribution towards the production costs of the book.
- Publishers can expect architectural practices to provide photography and imagery related to their work. Costs of securing photography rights or paying to have drawings re-sized or digitised can be significant and should be factored in at the beginning of the project.

Some commercial publishers have a strong brand

Some of the best-known architectural publishers have strong and distinctive brands; they stand out on the shelves as part of a family of books. Architectural practices can benefit by being associated with these big-name publishers, but

---

The publishing process for commercial books

1   The practice sends a publisher a proposal containing an outline of the book's basic aims and scope, its central themes, arguments, a summary of the kind of work or concepts it will be exploring and, where appropriate, a portfolio of work. Once accepted, the publisher issues a contract and, for the author, the lengthy work of collating information and writing the text begins.

2   A commissioning editor works with the practice to define the book's parameters in terms of content, scope and production specification.

3   Once written, the manuscript is handed over to a project editor who will see it through the processes of layouts, proofing, indexing, production and publication.

4   The publisher handles distribution and marketing. However, commercial publishers are also increasingly keen to use the practice's own PR mechanism, contacts and client lists to get the book the widest possible exposure.

they might need to consider whether they might benefit more from approaching a smaller-scale publisher who would create a bespoke design.

Lists and publishing brands do change

Commissioning editors have a significant influence on the body of work that they represent, and they may move on, so it is important to know and like a publisher's current list rather than simply going on past reputation.

Self-publishing

Methods of self-publishing range from books produced entirely in-house with every task, from design and writing to photography, undertaken by the architectural practice, to books which draw on the expertise of external agencies. Self-published books are not technically 'published' unless the practice decides to procure an ISBN.

See also: Technical issues, page 142

The internet, in particular, has opened up the mechanics of self-publishing so it is now possible to produce a simple book fairly cheaply. Internet publishing companies even offer a range of templates into which the user can load text and images online, removing some of the technical work of deciding how to lay out text and imagery on the page. Alternatively, the book can be designed and sent as a file over the internet in a wide range of formats.

Key characteristics of self-publishing are explored below.

The costs are for the practice to determine

A book produced entirely in-house and printed on demand over the internet might cost as little as £20 per copy, but the supplied volume might not meet expectations. On the other hand, a book designed and created by professionals using excellent paper and the best photography could cost £50,000 or more for a minimum print run. It is for the practice to control the budget.

The practice can undertake all tasks in-house or use external specialists

Self-publishing requires the architectural practice to take on the role of publisher as well as client. Managing the publication process and keeping the book true to its initial concept through each of the stages of its development is a skilled and time-consuming task which should not be underestimated. The practice may decide to hire the skills of specialists, including:

- a designer
- a photographer
- a writer
- an editor
- a proofreader
- an indexer
- PR consultants.

The publishing process for self-published books

1 The practice develops the concept – sometimes this initial thinking is undertaken with the input of a designer and an editor.
2 The design is created. Some architectural practices may take this on in-house, but many approach a design company.
3 Images, including photography, plans, diagrams and sketches, are gathered. Some technical contractual and permissions issues may arise, as explained in the section *Intellectual property*, page 142.
4 The text is created, either by the practice alone or with the input of a professional writer. Some practices generate their own text and employ an editor to help pull the content into a coherent written style.
5 Other work is taken on in-house or outsourced, including proofing, indexing and sourcing and compiling permissions and credits.
6 Frequently, the design company handles the printing; however, architectural practices may have their own connections or may wish to source independent quotations. Print costs can vary significantly depending on the method chosen (lithographic or digital, see page 145), the printer's set up, machinery and location. It can be cheaper to print overseas, although logistics and delivery times will need to be considered.
7 The practice will need to undertake any marketing work required. Self-published books have no publicity mechanism and no distribution network. If a practice secures an ISBN and wants to sell through bookshops and libraries, then negotiations will need to be handled by the practice, as will shipping and the monitoring of stock levels.

Self-publishing can be much quicker

If a practice knows the kind of book it wants to produce and is able to gather information and source material together readily, it can be much quicker to self-publish.

Storage and transportation

Warehousing and transportation logistics are further on-costs that may need to be factored into the overall publication cost.

Postage

The cost of postage needs to be factored into the budget with on-demand printing, with each order requiring postage to be paid. In traditional printing, where there is a single delivery, carriage is usually included in the price.

Technical issues

This section is intended as a quick summary of a specialist field. A practice publishing commercially will be able to rely on their publisher for more information, and self-publishing practices may be able to rely on their designer or printer. However, there are some issues which are essential to consider before embarking on the production of a book.

Intellectual property

Copyright

Books automatically qualify for copyright protection. However, to help protect the work, the book can carry the © symbol, the name of the copyright owner (an individual or company) and the year of publication. This lets others know when the term of protection started (and therefore whether it is still covered by copyright), it also indicates who to approach should they need to ask permission to use the work.

Credits and permissions

It is essential to ask permission to use other people's work. This can range from a polite request to a contract-fulfilling obligation. Permission to reproduce material must come from the actual holder of the copyright, and a full copyright notice needs to be printed in the book.

Photography contracts

Problems can arise when photographers and agencies include clauses in their contracts excluding the use of their images in publications. This can mean that a practice cannot use images which it has commissioned and paid for without paying again. It is not unheard of for these fees to match the proposed budget for the entire book in commercial publishing deals.

Imagery

Photography libraries

A wide range of images is available from photography libraries. The quality varies, as does the deal. Some are free (but require crediting), others will ask for detailed information about the print run, territories of publication and the size at which the image will be shown to calculate a price for using the photograph.

Drawings and plans

Re-sizing can cause problems, requiring drawings to be redrawn; similarly, drawings or sketches could need to be redrawn or digitised. Publishers expect design practices to fund the cost of this work.

Packaging

Paper stock

Three main factors have to be taken into account with regard to paper selection:

* weight – a book's perceived quality can be undermined by paper which is too light
* finish – digital printing needs a coated paper for the ink to take (see printing processes below) while lithographic printing offers more flexibility with paper stocks
* ecological paper – check for part-recycled to 100 per cent recycled, chlorine-free and FSC approved. Use of a particular specification can be flagged in the credits.

The cover

The options are hardback (with or without dust jacket) and softback (with optional folded flaps to give the cover additional structure). Remember to consider how the cover and text sheets will work together. An overly light cover stock might feel flimsy, while one which is too thick will make the book unwieldy and might result in excessive postage costs. The printer will advise what their press can handle and the cost differences. A 'dummy' will confirm whether or not the paper selected is appropriate.

The spine

Conventions for presenting the title differ. In the UK and the USA, titles are usually written top-to-bottom, while in continental Europe titles tend to be the other way round.

Binding

There is a range of methods on offer. Where images are printed across the middle of the book, consideration needs to be given to how flat the binding will allow the pages to be opened.

Hardbound books

With this method of binding, bundles of pages are sewn together and attached to rigid board covers.

Softbound books

Soft-binding involves three primary methods:

• Thermally activated (perfect) binding – pages are glued at the spine. Sometimes books do not spread wide with this method and can fall apart with repeated handling.
• Stitched or sewn binding – constructed as for a hardbound book, except with a soft cover. This is more expensive than perfect binding but is as durable as a hardbound book and allows the pages to be spread wide.
• Saddle-stitched binding: a set of nested folios is stapled in a magazine-style book. This is only suitable for slim editions.

Printing processes

There are two main methods of printing:

- Lithographic printing – a traditional process by which each colour is separated and printed separately, which is most economical for longer print runs.
- Digital printing – the ink is squirted onto the paper in a single process, making it suitable for short print runs.

ISBN and legal deposit

An International Standard Book Number (ISBN) is a product number used for ordering and listing books sold through bookshops. Booksellers cannot sell a book without one. ISBNs are acquired from the UK ISBN Agency, and the publisher is required to send a copy of the book to the British Library within one month of publication.

Conclusion

Architectural practices need high-quality visual materials to market their practice and communicate their work in a tough, fast-moving professional arena. Like designing a good building, producing a good book is a complex task and, as with any specialism, taking advice from the right consultants will produce a better product.

Standards in architectural publishing have never been higher. Trying to cut too many corners will show in the subtle things – a layout that does not flow, images which do not do a project justice, a paper stock which does not feel right or text which is dull. The general rule with publishing is that you get what you pay for; a beautiful book takes time and energy (and therefore money) to create. The solutions which work so perfectly and seem so simple have usually taken the most time and skill to achieve.

However, the bold and ambitious should not be deterred. Step changes in the technologies associated with publishing (design packages which are easier than ever to use and print techniques which have moved on immensely over the past ten years) have opened up a wide range of new publishing options. The way ahead is exciting, and architectural practices which thrive on innovation will find creative new ways of communicating their thinking.

SUMMARY

- Identify the target audience for the book from the outset and write for that audience alone, being clear about what it is hoped that the book will achieve.
- Clearly map out content to reflect the practice's vision for the book, ensuring that the time is right for the practice to publish.
- Identify budgets and deadlines at the start of the project as these will have a significant influence on the publication route selected.
- Research publishers and options – self-publishing or commercial publishing – weighing the advantages and costs of each against the anticipated return.

Section 11
Writing skills for marketing collateral

Helen Elias, *AECOM*

Websites, brochures and project sheets, along with submission and bid documents, form the backbone of the way that architects communicate to a wide and diverse range of audiences. Other forms of written materials that may also need to be developed during any one year are legion – ranging from presentations and reports to professional developers and clients through to liaising with private clients and the general public.

Developing the written content for any resource that is to communicate effectively on behalf of the practice (whether in print or online) is an important task – and one that is often underestimated. Those first few words in an item of marketing collateral, such as a brochure or on a website, are key to grabbing and maintaining the attention of a reader. Get the tone and voice of that first piece of written information wrong, and that crucial chance to communicate the values and abilities of the practice will be gone, possibly for good.

Writing the website and marketing materials

Different approaches are needed to develop written content for print and online use.

Writing for the web

Designing and delivering a website is a complex process. Once the decision is made to develop a website for the practice, it is all too easy to get carried away and focus on what the site is going to look like, and any special interactive functionality that can be used to engage the visitor and make the site memorable. It will matter not one jot how clever or beautiful the website looks if the written content does not match the expectations set by the visual appearance. Boring or clumsy text is still going to be boring or clumsy, whatever the context of its presentation.

However, before creating and uploading a website about the practice, it is important to plan exactly what content is required. Thoroughly considering the audience or target market, as well as defining the purpose of the site, will inform the content to be developed. Follow this simple process to deliver an end result that both meets the aspirations of the people working for the practice and sends the right visual and written messages to the wider audience. A website is one of the key tools that will communicate the brand and reputation of the firm. Get this wrong, and the entire reputation of the practice can be undermined.

"A website is one of the key tools that will communicate the brand and reputation of the firm."

Start by identifying all the audiences likely to visit the site, which can include:

- existing clients
- potential clients
- friends and family
- architectural students
- potential employees
- the casual web browser
- a specific searcher
- journalists.

Defining the audiences will allow development of understanding about what the different visitors to the site are looking for – and will drive the overall tone of the site and its characteristics. This will allow the content of the site to be organised according to the expectations of the visitors. This organisation could well differ from the instinctive wish to jump straight into showcasing the work and skills of the practice. A well thought through site will recognise that potential clients have a problem or a need, and will present its approach in terms of problem-solving; saving clients time and money while developing design solutions that will truly help the client organisation, with new buildings developed that will add value to the business case, whatever the end use. Sites that merely present catalogues of work are not going to communicate problem-solving and creativity – the less tangible, but essential, assets of any practice.

Organise the information to be presented on the site into categories, selected according to visitor needs. Each category requires a snappy title, as this will become a link to a specific section on the site.

A quick check of websites from competitor practices will show the way that other firms cluster messages and information. Frequently used categories from architectural practice sites include:

• Sectors, Where we work, Theory
• Services, What we do, Skills, Teams
• About us, Our people, Meet the team, Practice
• Values, Mission, Culture, Data
• Projects, Experience
• Press, News, Awards, Publications
• Contact us, Contact
• Career, Futures, Opportunities
• Blog, Sign up, Newsletters, Downloads.

Once the site has been planned in detail, writing the content for each section and individual pages can take place within a more organised structure. This will allow repetition to be avoided.

When writing for websites, it is important to remember the following:

• *Reader attention span* – it is more difficult to read material on screen than on a page. Coupled with this, visitors to web pages generally have shorter attention spans. Users of websites are notoriously impatient, wanting to get to the information quickly, stay active and get things done. No one wants to trawl through pages of PR puff. Keep text short, crisp and to the point. Web text must be punchy and direct to engage the reader.
• *Keep it relevant* – make sure all the information on each page is useful. Think hard about the material presented. Detailed technical information is not always the right content to put onto a web page presenting the work of a firm of architects. Project information explaining the problems faced and the solution, with any sustainable or design approach facts thrown in, will be of more interest.

- *Don't be technical* – be specific about services offered and the capability of the practice. A cardinal rule of writing for the wider audience is never to assume prior knowledge. Do not expect the visitor to be aware of all the professional skills that the firm can offer.
- *Stay friendly* – web pages tend to be more casual than printed brochures. It is fine to have a more relaxed, informal writing style – generating a friendly tone will make the site more approachable, less formal. Friendly writing makes for an easy read. However, be careful not to overdo it, as too chatty a website can be off-putting within the professional services sector.
- *Keep it short and to the point* – the firm's website is not the place for a long-winded dissertation, yet at the same time reading on a screen tends to be a slower process for most people than reading from a page. Website readers tend to scan a page rather than read in depth – so perhaps up to 20 per cent of the information on a page will be absorbed. Cutting text into chunks and using cross-headings and bullet points will help readers skimming the page for specific information. Readers are drawn to keywords. Scatter words that reflect aspiration – creativity, sustainability – throughout the pages.
- *Key messages first* – visitors to a web page usually cast two horizontal sweeps of the eye across the page, and then one vertical sweep down the left-hand side. Most readers will not interrogate text in great detail on a first visit, when a shortlist might be being drawn up comparing different sites. So it is important to get key messages about the practice into the first two paragraphs on the page, as these are the pieces of text most likely to be read.
- *Use bullet points to get information across quickly* – remember that users do not like to have to scroll down a page to complete reading an item – another reason to keep information short. Use key words on cross-headings to help the reader navigate quickly to the information being sought.
- *Cut out the welcoming introduction* – 'Welcome to our site' text is irritating and can be a barrier, prompting visitors to leave the site without looking any further.
- *Keywords* – identify keywords that people will use in search engines, to drive traffic to the site, and make sure that these words appear regularly within the content.

Writing brochures and other marketing materials

Writing a brochure, a leaflet, a mail shot, a flyer, a report, a submission or anything else that is going to communicate in print the design approach and solutions of the practice, takes just as much planning and thought as developing the text for the practice's website. A brochure has a clear job to do: it has to engage with a targeted reader and persuade that person to think positively about the practice. In marketing terms, the brochure has got to make that first impression about the practice. If it is visually uninspiring, and a dull read, the impression made will not be favourable.

Producing a new brochure is time consuming and expensive. To get the most from the end product, any new marketing resource must be designed and developed with the reader in mind. Client-facing materials are all about presenting the practice as a viable operator that is within the client's own comfort zone, not bombarding the reader with jargon and detailed practice or discipline technicalities. Remember that a brochure is a piece of frontline collateral, used during the early stages when developing a relationship with a new client. It is, first and foremost, a sales tool.

Audience

Start by identifying exactly what the piece of marketing collateral is going to be asked to do. If the practice is small, a simple brochure that sets out design approach, culture and examples of a few projects might be fine. By the time the firm has grown, includes regional offices and is delivering work across many sectors, a one-size-fits-all brochure might not be appropriate – and will also be a more costly item to produce.

- Consider all routes to presenting the work of the firm – it may be that a smaller leaflet for each sector targeted, and another leaflet focusing on design approach and technical services offered, may be more appropriate.
- Be clear about the audiences that the product being developed will be sent to and how the brochure will be used. The average reading time for a company brochure is about nine seconds – so the finished product really has to work hard to make an impact. A good brochure is a careful combination of design and key messages, meticulously constructed to present an instant snapshot of the firm.

Keep it high level

Avoid the temptation to write a navel-gaze, talking exclusively about the technical skills on offer in the practice. Highlighting what the firm can do is undoubtedly within the comfort zone for the firm itself. However, consider what the reader – the potential client – wants to know, and put those needs first. Make the person reading the text feel that their problems will be listened to and understood and that a solution will be provided. Invariably, clients need reassurance that their project vision is going to be delivered on time and to budget. This information must come first, as the opening paragraphs are more likely to be read than any other part of the brochure, apart from the address and phone number. Remember that, when looking at each page in the brochure, potential clients are going to be considering the information presented in terms of how it will relate to themselves.

Avoid technical jargon

The practice may operate any number of software packages and have complex technical abilities that aid working processes. This level of information may be appropriate in a detailed submission document, but that degree of communication is a long way down the line. In a front-end brochure, which is introducing the client to the practice, it is not necessary to go into that much detail about technology. When writing any form of marketing collateral, always write from the reader's point of view.

Cut the history

One of the most comfortable places for an non-professional writer to begin a company brochure is by launching into the founding date and aspiration of the practice. Avoid wasting time and precious space on information that is not conveying a benefit. A brochure that begins 'Aspirational Architects was founded in 2002 by Bob Borage and Emma Castle...' is not going to engage any reader. It is more likely that text beginning this way will act as a barrier. Clients will be more engaged by an opening statement which clearly states that the practice helps client organisations to be successful.

Keep it short

A brochure of more than eight pages might well need a contents page. It is asking a lot of a casual reader to have to navigate their way through a sales document. If a planned piece of collateral looks as if is going to be 12 or 16 pages long, take a long hard look at it and edit the text. Is all that information really needed?

The central messages

An effective brochure will present just a few core central messages in a logical, compelling way. Avoid introducing too many points at once and ensure that all potential benefits are linked in to the central message.

Less is more

There is no need to pack every surface of the brochure with text. Give images and copy room to communicate. A badly designed brochure, over-stuffed with information, is not going to do the practice any favours.

Diagrams are good

Some issues are complex, and trying to express an architectural design approach or vision can run the risk of sounding pretentious. Consider expressing ideas and concepts diagrammatically. A colourful mind-map or diagram will communicate complex thinking more easily than a wordy explanation.

Images

Invest in professional photography, if the firm can afford it. A well-taken image will do more to present the firm's work than the quick snapshot taken by the project architect. If the practice has not built anything, populate the marketing resource with drawings, diagrams and generic images.

Use captions

The captions to the images are going to be read more than any other part of the brochure. Use this opportunity wisely. Captions can present a clever solution, a piece of creativity, a benefit to a client, sector knowledge, regional spread or technical expertise. Try to ensure that the captions reflect the key messages of the brochure, and the practice overall.

Contact details

Make sure that the address, contact details and numbers are easy to find and up to date.

Writing tips

When developing written content, it is important to present information in a consistent written style. Some of the same underlying principles apply across the board, whatever resource is being developed. One way to achieve consistency in written collateral across a busy firm of architects, all of whom will be producing content at one time or another, is to establish a style guide for the practice.

"establish a style guide for the practice"

Style guide

Policing written materials is easy when the firm is small but is not so easy to control once the practice starts to grow. Written style, in terms of grammar and punctuation, can easily become inconsistent across materials developed by different authors. Many practices therefore find it helpful to develop an in-house style guide as a reference tool, giving set answers to frequently occurring grammatical and style issues.

See also:
Manuals,
page 77

Suggestions for how to tackle a few of the more common pitfalls that arise during developing written text about architecture and the built environment are given in a basic style guide in Appendix 3. This is by no means a definitive list, but it is at least a start. Some written issues can be very much a matter of personal choice. Making a decision and then sticking to it across all communication materials will allow development of written resources to a consistent standard.

There are plenty of useful guides to English grammar, available both online and through bookshops. An investment in a guide will be invaluable to anyone embarking on a role as practice copywriter.

In conclusion, developing the written content of resources needs a considered and strategic approach. Materials that present the practice to its markets should do so clearly and convincingly.

SUMMARY

- Different approaches are needed to develop written content for print and online use.
- Identify the target audience.
- Include key messages to grab readers' attention.
- Be consistent across all materials, introducing a style guide as the firm grows.
- Keep content high level, avoid technical talk and jargon and offer problem-solving possibilities.
- Use diagrams, particularly professional images, which have enormous impact.
- Captions are a great way to add extra information as their text will be read more carefully by the reader.

Appendix 1

PRESS RELEASE

Dramatic cantilevered glass staircase for Grade II listed building

- Installation within Grade II listed manor house
- First use of cantilevered beam detail in UK residential project

A unique glass staircase which maximises transparency and incorporates lighting has been installed at Blewbury Manor, an historic Grade II listed house near Didcot, Oxfordshire.

Spratley Studios worked with Scottish-based glass specialist designers IPIG (Inspired Projects In Glass) to develop the single flight of structural glass stairs and landing space which now link the central living area to the upper floor within the house.

Delivering a sophisticated contemporary staircase within the constraints of the historic listed seventeenth-century building required careful negotiation with both English Heritage and Vale of White Horse Conservation Department. The installation achieves a distinctive architectural dialogue, using materials to link the traditional and the contemporary with the historic core of the manor house.

The complete design successfully complements the original striking features of the building and the insertion of a dramatic arched glass roof enclosing the medieval courtyard, internal reconfiguration and the suspended glass staircase complete an exceptional living space.

Curved glass roof structure enclosing medieval courtyard
Remaining true to the central medieval courtyard was a priority in our resolve, as was remaining honest to the original ambience of the space.

The insertion of the glass roof gave a modern interpretation of the original medieval courtyard.

The design seeks to be as transparent as possible, creating an ambience of inside out and retaining the initial character. The integrity of new technology enhances the listed building as a forward looking piece of its time.

With the central hub of the home a medieval courtyard, it was only natural for this space to contain the kitchen. Retaining the courtyard ambience, the solution included a curved glass roof. A finely detailed curved glass roof structure on stainless steel curved rafters, bespoke to fit the aperture, was inserted over the existing central portion of the courtyard.

These sleek, glazed bespoke intrusions are to be transparent, reflective of the water that characterises the landscape but also enabling the retained listed structures to stand out and remain on view. Conversion of the central medieval courtyard was carefully and sympathetically thought through and eagerly approved by the council's conservation team.

The structural principles of the staircase
The staircase design solution sees the first use of a cantilevered glass beam to support a structural glass landing in a residential project.

The staircase is formed of a combination of structural glass elements, fixed to, and built into, the fabric of the building. A single laminated glass panel acts as both stringer and balustrade. This panel both supports, and is braced by, structural glass treads. The treads are simply supported between the glass stringer panel and a fabricated steel side plate, which also accommodates fibre optic lighting heads.

The laminated glass balustrade spans 3.7m from a simple shoe floor connection to a support at first floor level. It is stabilised by a rigid connection at the landing and by the treads which "tie" the stringer to the wall to prevent the panel from buckling.

Half of the load of the staircase is supported on a single, laminated glass beam which cantilevers 1.1m from the wall at first floor level. The same beam also provides support to the balcony floor panel and balcony balustrade. The floor, balustrade and secondary beam elements are all located within fabricated stainless steel channels built into the walls prior to plastering and glass installation.

The glass floor and treads were treated with an applied surface finish, fired into the glass to provide slip resistance and visual highlights to the treads. The glass floor, panel and treads comprise three layers of 10mm toughened low iron glass, laminated with PVB interlayers. At night, 48 fibre optic heads, contained within the wall to give single or changing light, illuminate the treads from within.

The staircase sees the first use of a glass cantilevered beam detail in a residential project. The glass beam comprises three layers of 12mm toughened low iron glass, laminated with PVB interlayers. Careful co-ordination with the primary steelwork was needed to ensure adequate structural support could be achieved in such an historic building.

The stringer and balustrade panels and secondary beam beneath the glass floor comprise two layers of 12mm toughened low iron glass, laminated with PVB interlayers.

The staircase was designed, engineered and installed by IPIG, based on a concept by Spratley Studios.

The fibre optic lighting was designed and installed by IPIG and supplied by Universal Fibre Optics.

The End

Word Count: 726

Project team

Architects	Spratley Studios
Glass Roof and Staircase Designer	IPIG (Inspired Projects In Glass)
Contractor	Boshers
Structural Engineer	Elliot Wood

For further information or photographs please contact:

Spratley Studios	Trudy Evans
	trudy@spratley.co.uk
	Tel: 01491 411277

For further information on Spratley Studios please visit www.spratley.co.uk

Notes to editor

Spratley Studios is a practice of creative architects and designers based in Henley-on-Thames, Oxon. The practice has a diverse project base including unique one-off private builds, commercial residential, business park development, leisure industry and educational sector. A fundamental belief in the value of good design inspires us to test and challenge the opportunities of each project. This approach has resulted in the practice receiving a variety of awards including two of our offices being regionally shortlisted for the British Council of Offices Award in 2008.

Goodwood Rise	**RIBA Ibstock Downland Prize: Best Small Project 2005**
Cherrytree Barn	**RIBA South Conservation Award: Commendation 2006**
	RIBA Ibstock Downland Prize; Shortlisted 2006
174 Milton Park	**RIBA Ibstock Downland Prize; Shortlisted 2007**
St. Francis Chapel	**Sussex Heritage Award Public Building Winner 2007**
	NMT Nursery Design Winner 2007
South60	**British Council of Offices Award Regional Shortlisted 2008**
Cedarwood	**British Council of Offices Award Regional Shortlisted 2008**

Reproduced by kind courtesy of Trudy Evans, Spratley Studios.

Picture credit (page 157): Nick Kane, © Spratley Studios.

Appendix 2
Architecture and design award schemes

This is by no means a definitive list of the many current award schemes which could be of interest to a practice of architects. Market sector and client industries will all have award schemes that may present opportunities for further recognition for the practice. A complete and up-to-date version of this list is available on the RIBA website, at www.architecture.com/Awards/OtherArchitecturalAwards/

ACE/RIBA Award for Religious Architecture http://acetrust.org

AIA London/UK Excellence in Design Awards http://aiauk.org

AJ Small Projects Award www.architectsjournal.co.uk

AR Awards for Emerging Architecture www.arplus.com

Art Fund (formerly the Gulbenkian) Prize for Museums and Galleries www.artfundprize.org.uk

Autodesk Revit User Design Awards www.autodesk.co.uk

BD Architect of the Year Awards www.bdonline.co.uk

Brick Awards www.brick.org.uk

British Construction Industry Awards www.bciawards.org.uk

British Council for Offices Awards www.bco.org.uk

British Council of Shopping Centres Town Centre Environment Awards www.bcsc.org.uk

British Urban Regeneration Association (BURA) Awards www.bura.org.uk

Building Better Healthcare Awards www.bbhealthcare.co.uk

Building for Life Awards www.buildingforlife.org

Civic Building of the Year Award www.scala.org.uk

Civic Trust Awards www.civictrustawards.org.uk

Concrete Society Awards www.concrete.org.uk

Europa Nostra Awards www.europanostra.org

European Prize for Urban Public Space www.architecturefoundation.org.uk

Grand Designs Magazine Awards www.granddesignsmagazine.com

Green Apple Environmental Awards www.thegreenorganisation.info

Green Awards www.greenawards.co.uk

Housebuilding Innovation Awards www.hbmedia.co.uk

Housing Design Awards www.designforhomes.org

International Property Awards www.propertyawards.net

John Betjeman Award www.spab.org.uk

LABC National 'Built in Quality' Awards www.labc.uk.com

MIPIM Awards www.mipim.com

Philip Webb Award www.spab.org.uk

Pritzker Architecture Prize www.pritzkerprize.com

RIBA Awards www.architecture.com

RICS Awards www.rics.org

RTPI Planning Awards www.rtpi.org.uk

Stirling Prize www.architecture.com

Structural Awards www.istructe.org

Structural Steel Design Awards www.steelconstruction.org

UK Housing Awards www.cih.org

Urbanism Awards www.academyofurbanism.org.uk

Appendix 3
Basic style guide for architects

Abbreviations/acronyms An acronym is an abbreviation that is spoken as a word, rather than as the individual letters (e.g. NATO, Unison, Aid, rather than BBC, EU, UK)

The first time that the name of an organisation is used, write it out in full, with the abbreviation in brackets. After that, the abbreviation can be used throughout the rest of the text:

* use: 'Sarah Brown is a member of the Royal Institute of British Architects (RIBA)'
* avoid: 'Sarah Brown is a member of the RIBA (Royal Institute of British Architects)'.

Affect/effect 'To affect' means to have an influence on or to change ('It affected me deeply'). 'To effect' means to bring about or to cause ('This approach can effect great changes').

Ampersand Wherever possible, avoid the use of '&' in written text. Use only when it appears as part of the verified name of an organisation (e.g. B&Q, Marks & Spencer).

And, but Try to avoid starting a sentence with 'And' or 'But'. Try using 'In addition' or 'However' instead.

Apostrophes Apostrophes are used to:

* take the place of missing letters in contractions: don't (do not), wouldn't (would not) and it's (it is)
* denote ownership.

If the thing or person you are writing about is singular and the word does not end in 's', add an apostrophe followed by 's': 'Sarah Brown's report', 'today's meeting', 'the project's deadline'.

Where a singular word or name ends in 's', the word would usually also take an apostrophe followed by 's', but be guided by pronunciation and use a plural apostrophe (after the 's') where it helps: 'the boss's hat'.

The apostrophe is placed after the 's' to indicate ownership to more than one thing or person, 'the clients' feedback', 'the architects' training programme'. The exception is when a plural noun ends in a letter other than 's': 'the children's party' and 'the gentlemen's hats').

The possessive apostrophe is used in phrases such as 'four years' research', '200 hours' teamwork'.

Do not use apostrophes in decades: 'the 1960s', not 'the 60's'

Book/report titles   Italicise titles of books, journals or reports rather than underlining or using quote marks to indicate a publication.

Brackets   (If the brackets enclose the whole sentence, the full stop goes inside.) If only the last part of the sentence is in brackets, put the full stop outside (like this).

Brownfield   Also 'greenfield' (not 'brown-field' or 'green-field').

Bullet points   Where bullet points are preceded by an introductory sentence, the sentence should end in a colon:

• each bullet point should begin with a capital or lower case letter, according to preference, but be consistent
• do not indent bullet points
• do not use any punctuation at the end of each point (such as commas, semi-colons or full stops) *except* for the last bullet point, which should end with a full stop
• the first sentence within a bullet point should end with a full stop. The second one should not – unless the bullet point is the last one in the list.

Capital letters   As a general rule, avoid using capital letters. Some writers frequently give capital letters to job titles and other words such as client, project and company. This is grammatically incorrect as these words are not proper nouns.

- Some common pitfalls include:
- 'architect' not 'Architect'
- 'the world' not 'the World'
- 'structural engineer' not 'Structural Engineer'
- 'report' not 'Report'
- 'company' not 'Company'
- 'client' not 'Client'
- 'firm' not 'Firm'.

Collective nouns   Use a singular verb for the name of the practice and any other organisation. ('Smith Architects has announced', not 'Smith Architects have announced'.)

Commas   Commas indicate the end of a phrase, or, alternatively, a pause for breath. Commas can also be used instead of brackets.

Currencies   Use lower case when spelling out currencies, e.g. US 'dollars', British 'pounds'. Also, 'euro' remains lower case and does not have a plural form: '1 euro', '50 euro', 'one million euro' (€).

Dates and times   (UK format) Number first, then month and year, not separated by a comma. Do not add 'th', 'rd', 'nd' or 'st' to the number.

'29 September 2010', not September 29th, 2010' or '29th September, 2010'.

Do not abbreviate the month: 'September' not 'Sept', etc.

Use lower case for 'a.m.' and 'p.m.' in times (8.00 a.m., 7.00 p.m. but 12 noon).

Decimal numbers   Show decimal numbers to two places, with a digit before the decimal point: '0.75' not '.75'.

Different from   not 'different to' or 'different than'.

e.g.   not 'EG' 'E.G.' 'eg:' 'E.g.'

etc.   not 'Etc' 'Etc.' 'etc'.

Fractions   Write fractions out and use a hyphen, thus 'two-thirds', 'four-fifths', 'nine-tenths', not '2/3', '4/5' or '9/10'.

Full stops   One keyboard space is all that is needed between a full stop and the next sentence. Two spaces will create clumsy gaps between sentences. If a sentence ends with a question mark or an exclamation mark, it does not need a full stop as well.

Honours and qualifications   Use established abbreviations. There is no need for full stops between letters: 'RIBA' not 'R.I.B.A.'.

Numbers   Spell out full numbers from one to ten. From 11 to 999,999 use numbers (note the comma).

The exceptions are measurements and cash amounts: '6kg' '5 miles' '£8'.

From 1,000,000 upwards use 'one million', '11 million', 'two billion', '11 billion' etc. (but for cash amounts use '£5m' and '£20bn').

First, second, third – spell out up to ninth, then '10th', '21st', 'millionth' (no gap).

Percentages   In written text use 'per cent' not '%'. The % symbol can, however, be used in tables and graphs.

Public titles   Upper case, e.g. 'President', 'Her Majesty the Queen', 'Prime Minister', 'MP', 'Lord Mayor'.

Further reading

Birren, F. (1970). 'The elements of color'; in J. Itten, *The Art of Color*. John Wiley & Sons Inc.

Cooper, A. (1999). *The Inmates Are Running the Asylum*. SAMS.

Drew, J.T. and Meyer, S.A. (2003). *Color Management*. Rotovision.

Elias, H. (2006). *Effective Press Relations for the Built Environment: A Practical Guide*. Taylor & Francis.

Gerstner, K. (1964). *Designing Programmes*. Arthur Niggli Ltd.

Henrion, F.H.K. and Parkin, A. (1967). *Design Coordination and Corporate Image*. Studio Vista; Reinold Publishing Corporation.

Jannuzzi, M. and Smith, R. (2000). *Dotlinepixel: Thoughts On Cross-Media Design*. GCE Directions.

Lawrence, C. (2008). *Brands: Law, Practice and Precedents*. Jordans.

Oliver, S. (2001). *Public Relations Strategy*. Kogan Page.

Simpson, M., Padmore, J. and Taylor, N. (2005). 'Marketing in SMEs', Discussion Paper no 2005.08, University of Sheffield Management School.

Walker, K., Ferguson, C. and Denvir, P. (1998). *Creating New Clients: Marketing and Selling Professional Services*. Cassell.

Walker, K., Ferguson, C. and Denvir, P. (2000). *Managing Key Clients: Securing the Future of the Professional Services Firm*. Cassell.

Web resources

'BrandChannel: Glossary' available at
www.brandchannel.com/education_glossary. asp

'Case studies: How to find and work with a designer' available at
www.designcouncil.org.uk/Case-Studies/All-Case-Studies/Finding-and-working-
with-a-designer/

Index

Note: page numbers in italics refer to figures and tables